ICEBERG
Philanthropy

Unlocking Extraordinary Gifts
From Ordinary Donors

Fraser Green, CFRE
Beth McDonald, CFRE
Jose van Herpt, CFRE

Library and Archives Canada Cataloguing in Publication

Green, Fraser, 1956-
    Iceberg philanthropy : unlocking extraordinary gifts from ordinary donors / Fraser Green, Beth McDonald, Jose van Herpt.

ISBN 978-1-4196-6991-0

    1. Fund raising. 2. Nonprofit organizations--Finance.
I. McDonald, Beth, 1944- II. Van Herpt, Jose, 1960- III. Title.

HV41.2.G74 2007   361.7'630681   C2007-904130-2

ISBN-13: 978-1-4196-6991-0
ISBN-10: 1-4196-6991-5

Book design and layout by Bart Hawkins Kreps.
Front cover photo-illustration created by Bart Hawkins Kreps from a photo © Ralph A. Clevenger/CORBIS.

Manufactured by BookSurge Publishing in the United States of America.

Published in Canada by
The FLA Group Inc.
620-265 Carling Avenue
Ottawa, Ontario   K1S 2E1

In our hearts and minds always ...

We dedicate this book to the memory of the late Fran Lowe.

To us, Fran was a sister, a mentor, a friend and a business partner. Her incredible warmth and interest in others touched people's lives wherever she went.

Fran established the company that would become The FLA Group. Her vision was a consultancy built firmly on the pillars of research, teaching, fairness and transparency. Truth, unwavering values and the highest ethics were Fran's constant guides.

This book is the latest chapter of Fran's legacy and she'd be proud to know her daughter, Julie, helped with the research. We think she'd approve of its creativity, passion and genuine love of the donors and volunteers who make our sector such a wonderful place to work.

Thanks Fran, for inspiring this journey.

Jose van Herpt, CFRE
Principal
The FLA Group Inc.

Contents

Introduction

What's in a title?

This is a book about philanthropy. There's half your explanation.

It's also about a kind of philanthropy that's going to become awfully, awfully big over the next 20 years. Icebergs are awfully big too. Icebergs are usually triangular-shaped. So are fundraising pyramids.

We're going to tease you a bit here and not reveal the entire metaphor right now. But read on, gentle reader, and we'll explain ourselves fully in due course.

The big hairy idea

There are two big ideas actually:

- ◆ The first idea is that many of your most ordinary donors will make extraordinary gifts in the latter stages of their earthly lifetimes. In fact, their extraordinary gifts will in many cases be much, much bigger than the sum total of their lifetime giving.

- ◆ The second big idea is one of synergy – or fusion, if you prefer. From the fundraiser's perspective, this book is about an approach that effectively marries major gift strategy with direct marketing tactics. If you approach this idea with an open mind, we're pretty sure you'll be excited about its potential. If you're too "schooled" in your particular fundraising discipline (be it direct marketing or planned giving), your head might hurt a bit. We apologize in advance for any cranial pain we might cause.

Who this book is written for

We wrote this book with a very definite audience in mind. It's intended for those who have a direct and keen interest in raising more funds for the charity or cause that they're most deeply involved with.

It's particularly targeted to anyone who raises money for a charity or cause that uses direct mail to build and maintain the base of its donor pyramid. If direct mail isn't a part of your tactical portfolio, we're confident that you can take much of what we say and apply it intelligently to your own particular situation. But, if you have a direct mail donor base, this book should be right up your alley.

Professional fundraisers – especially development directors, direct marketing specialists and planned giving officers — will find it particularly useful, we hope.

It's also aimed at the volunteer – especially the Board Chair, the Treasurer, the Chair of the Fundraising Committee and board members in general. Iceberg Philanthropy in most cases will be executed and managed by staff. But, in almost all cases, it will have to be mandated by boards or their committees. We hope that this book will help board members understand the approach – and buy into it with enthusiasm.

What rookie preachers are taught

Legend has it that would-be preachers in seminary school are always given a basic lesson in writing and delivering sermons. That lesson goes something like this:

Tell them what you're going to tell them.
Tell them.
Then tell them what you've just told them.

So we'd now like to tell you what we're going to tell you:

- ◆ Chapter 1 talks about how complex, competitive and difficult today's charitable marketplace really is – both for the fundraiser and the donor. We think it's critical to truly understand your environment before planning strategy. So we start with a no-holds-barred description of the environment you're working in today.

- ◆ Chapter 2 talks about the relationship between the various categories of giving (we identify four) and the three categories of soliciting charitable funds. We align the traditional methods of giving with their corresponding fundraising tactics. Then we draw a diagonal line, where only parallel had previously existed, that is both fascinating and exciting.

- ◆ Next we go back to the literature and review the motivation for giving to charity – albeit from traditional sources. This is the stuff you'd be expected to know as you prepare for your Certified Fund Raising Executive exam. Knowing why donors give is every bit as important as knowing how donors give. In Chapter 3 we focus on why.

◆ Then in Chapter 4 we depart once again from conventional wisdom and think a bit outside the box about donor motivation. Here we examine the donor as an emotional – rather than rational – animal. Emotions, as you'll soon see, play a critical role in Iceberg Philanthropy.

◆ Now the fun really starts. In Chapter 5 we'll get close up and personal with that very ordinary direct mail donor who's going to leave you that extraordinary gift. We've been doing quantitative and qualitative research on this subject for years. And for the first time ever, we'll bring this donor fully to life and introduce you to her or him.

◆ Chapter 6 is also very much about research findings. Here we'll show you in some detail just how much money is in the legacy iceberg – and hopefully whet your appetite to want to earn some of it!

◆ In Chapter 7 we shift fully from the big picture and the conceptual to putting some real rubber on the road. We'll begin to walk you through the process of actually doing Iceberg Philanthropy. In keeping with the strategy of major gift fundraisers, our first step is prospect identification.

◆ When we first started doing conference presentations and articles in fundraising journals a few years ago, we created a bit of a stir about how "the planned giving industry" goes about its business. Our approach earned us the nickname of "planned giving contrarians". We wore that label as a badge of honour. Chapter 8 focuses on the two principles that underpin Iceberg Philanthropy. Contrarians we were called then – and contrarians we proudly remain!

◆ Next in Chapter 9 we'll outline a logical and sequential campaign-style approach that you can use to market Iceberg Philanthropy to your direct mail donor constituency. We've tried to make it specific enough for you to use – yet general enough for you to fit to your own specific needs. We think we've struck the right balance.

◆ Chapter 10 could well be the most practical and useful part of the book for you. We think it will be the chapter you'll return to and refer to most often. It contains 19 tried and true tips that will help ensure that your donor communications around legacy giving will have the desired effect. And, rest assured, these tips come straight from the donor's mouth. We didn't make any of this stuff up!

◆ Anyone with any sales training or experience knows all about customer objections. We know that donors considering legacy gifts almost invariably find themselves saying, "This is a great idea, but ...." To succeed, you'll need to take care of those buts. We'll show you how in Chapter 11.

◆ Chapter 12 is a reality check. Once we have you all excited about Iceberg Philanthropy and the revenue potential it offers, we're going to ask you to take a long hard look in the mirror and ask yourself if you're *really* ready to do this. You might not enjoy reading this chapter all that much because it will probably make you think about the various weaknesses and dysfunctions in your organization. Better you fix what you can before you start our journey. Everyone, especially your donors, will be better off in the long run if you do.

◆ Finally in Chapter 13 we'll take a close look at the whole issue of why most donors choose not to tell you when they make a charitable bequest to your organization. We'll share a newly created benchmark that comes from our research – and suggest ways in which you may be able to get more donors to open up and inform you about their legacy gifts.

Last but not least, this book has a conclusion. In that final section, we'll tell you what we just told you – just in case you need reminding!

How to use this book

This book is laid out chapter by chapter in a very linear fashion. Each chapter sets the stage for the one to follow. So we recommend that you read it from front to back and resist the urge to jump around too much.

If you find the first three or four chapters a bit disjointed, please keep in mind that they form the base for what is to come. And trust us that your patience will be rewarded. We're pretty sure you'll be fully engaged by Chapter 5 – if not before.

Once you've read it through once, you'll then be able to quickly access the chapter that can help you with the task at hand – whether it's prospect identification, working on next year's budget or writing a piece for your next donor newsletter. We hope this book will become a reference tool that you'll return to often.

So there you have it. Your orientation session is complete. Let's put on our gumboots, get into the boat – and go look at some big honkin' icebergs!

Chapter One
"It's a jungle in here"

Welcome to the scrum

In politics, a scrum is pretty much a daily event. A scrum is when a politician is surrounded by reporters and cameras and microphones – and the questions just come flying, many at the same time. A political scrum is really an impromptu press conference without any rules. It's unpredictable mayhem. Journalists love scrums. Politicians and their advisors tend to hate them.

In rugby the scrum is the part of the game where everyone bends over and grabs a person on either side – and one team tries to push the other team away from the ball that's somewhere on the ground.

Today's donor is simply overwhelmed. She feels as if she's being scrummed by all the good causes out there. The world of fundraising today is crowded. Very, very crowded. There are more charities and more causes asking more often in more different ways than ever before. The charitable marketplace is a noisy busy place where everyone feels jostled and bumped and pushed.

Think of it. There are some 82,000 registered charities in Canada today – and that number grows every year. Add to that the 80,000 charities and causes that aren't registered and you've got one helluva crowd.

How in the world is the poor donor supposed to keep track?

And not only are there a lot of charities asking today, they're asking in a lot of different ways:

- direct mail
- product sales
- dinners and golf tournaments
- pledge-a-thons
- lotteries and bingos
- car washes
- e-mail appeals
- calling you at suppertime
- infomercials on TV
- newspaper ads
- billboards
- door-to-door canvass
- stopping you on the street

The list goes on and on. But we're not done. Just look around the corner at what's coming next. Communications technology is just beginning to offer new methods of making charitable donations. That door-to-door canvasser who rings your bell can issue a receipt from a hand-held device. You can text message your Visa number over your cell phone. The market simply continues to fragment to suit the individual donor's tastes.

The evolution gap

To understand what's going on in the world today, it's useful to start from an evolutionary perspective.

As a species, we humans are pretty much the same beings we were two millenniums ago. Okay, we're taller and we have better teeth. But our minds and hearts and souls haven't changed much at all in the past couple of thousand years.

People have about the same innate ability to process incoming information as our Mesopotamian ancestors did.

But what about the evolution of communications technology? That's another story entirely.

Our ability to broadcast messages has exploded in the last half century. But our ability to receive them hasn't. That creates a huge gap between the messages we send and the messages we receive. Fundraisers need to understand this.

The speeding parade

Communications expert Bernard Gauthier likes to talk about the speeding parade. He likens communications to a parade. There are floats and bands and clowns – just like the parades you take your kids to.

Not that long ago, parades were simple affairs. You stood on the sidewalk and watched as a couple of dozen floats crawled by – and the bands and clowns walked past you in a pretty leisurely fashion.

Today the floats and bands are whizzing by at 160 kilometres an hour. They're a blur. And there are 4,000 floats in today's parade.

Four thousand floats at 160 kilometres an hour. How in the world do you keep track? You don't.

Worse yet, look at this parade from another vantage point.

You and your friends have decided to enter a float in the parade. You're hoping to win first prize as the "Best

New Float" in this year's event. After the parade, the audience will vote to select the winner.

Yet this parade is huge and it's terribly fast. How will the crowd even notice your float – let alone pick it as their favourite?

The float is your charity. The audience is your pool of donors and prospects. The other floats are your competition. The parade is a day in the life of your donor.

How will you win hearts and minds (not to mention dollars) in this hurricane of activity?

Advertising professionals estimate that the average person today is exposed to some 4,000 messages of a "marketing" nature. "Buy this. Think that. Vote for me. Donate to us. Stop that behaviour. Be aware of this problem. Fear my God."

And here's another pill for you to swallow. You're a fundraiser and, as such, you think a lot about your donors. Well, here's a newsflash. They're not donors. They're people.

They're parents and grandparents. They're lovers and friends. They're consumers. They're parishioners. They're citizens. They're neighbours. They're fans. They're a whole lot of things.

Make no mistake. You are after your donor's mind share. And you're not just competing with 160,000-plus other worthy causes out there. You're competing with the entire communications universe.

The generation gap is alive and well

Members of the Civic generation grew up during the 1930s and 1940s. Media in those days was the radio in the living room – and listening to Bing Crosby or The Shadow after supper.

We grew up in the fifties and sixties. We're a part of the Baby Boom generation. We grew up in the age of television. Mind you, we only had two channels – and everybody watched Ed Sullivan at 8 p.m. on Sunday nights.

Our kids, nieces and nephews are members of the Boom Echo generation. They've grown up in an age of the Internet, instant messaging, e-mail, call waiting, cellular technology, text messaging, 400 TV channels and satellite radio.

We confess to struggling to keep up with communications technology. Our new cell phones and digital cameras are a headache to figure out. But we do figure them out because we want to use them well.

Our kids pick up new technology the way they put on new socks. To them, it's a no-brainer.

Our parents' generation generally don't have e-mail accounts. They don't have cell phones. They don't have digital cameras. And our money says they'll never have these things. The Civic generation has gone as far down the technology highway as it's going to go.

Our parents resemble today's typical direct mail donor. They're older. They're retired. They simply can't or won't keep up with the dizzying change that's going on around them. They still listen to Frank Sinatra and they like black and white movies.

In his book *Boom, Bust & Echo*, David K. Foot makes the bold statement that "demographics is two-thirds of everything". He goes on to say, "Demography, the study of populations, is the most powerful – and most underutilized – tool we have to understand the past and foretell the future."

It's hard to disagree with him.

Bernie Gauthier, who we mentioned earlier, is the Vice President of Vision Research, a market research company based in Ottawa. When it comes to communications, messaging and targeting audiences Bernie is our go-to guy. He's simply brilliant.

We all like to think of Canada as this patchwork of regions – each with its own distinct culture and characteristics. We think of Cape Bretoners as being very different from, say, people from Southern Alberta ranch country.

Yet Bernie says that it's age that separates us. He maintains that if you took a cross-section of people of roughly the same age across the country and put them in a room for a focus group discussion, they'd sound surprisingly alike.

Yet, if you took a couple of those 70-somethings and had them watch a focus group discussion of 15-year-olds from across the country, they'd become confused very quickly. "What is she talking about, Lois?"

Demographers like to talk about generational cohorts. The Civic generation that was born before or during the Second World War. The Boomers born between 1946 and 1966. Then Gen X. Then the Boom Echo generation.

Iceberg Philanthropy is all about Civics. Our parents' generation. The strategy, tactics, methods and messages we're going to outline for you are all very much tailored to our parents' generation. These approaches wouldn't work on us. And they very likely wouldn't work on you. Please keep that in mind.

Our direct marketing mentor was the late Fran Lowe. One of the first things she told us (when we were clients of hers) was to write direct mail letter copy as if we were writing to an elderly aunt. Almost 20 years later, we still write that way.

The reason we're going on about this is simple. As you read on, you're probably going to react somewhat negatively to some of the strategies we'll outline. We simply ask you to try to remember that this isn't about you. It's about your Aunt Eileen – or whichever favourite aunt you choose (so long as she's over 60!).

The lemming effect

Human beings are highly social animals. We like to do things together. And we like to emulate the leaders in our social packs.

The vast majority of the human species follow conventional wisdom. Original thinkers among us are few and far between.

Not only that, the social pack usually makes it very hard for the original thinker to be heard. How did we treat Copernicus? Socrates? Nelson Mandela? Jesus?

Lemmings are a social species too. Except every so often, the leader of the pack takes everybody off a cliff.

As a fundraiser, are you an original thinker? Even some of the time? Even a little bit of the time? Or are you a lemming? If you're following the fundraising crowd, do you know where it's leading you?

Two lumberjacks

There's an old story we love about two lumberjacks who are cutting trees in the forest. Let's call them Larry and Luke.

> *Larry and Luke are expected to each cut 100 trees per day. As noon approaches one day, they've each only cut down 30 trees.*
>
> *Larry turns to Luke and grumbles, "Looks like I'll be working through lunch hour again."*
>
> *As the noon whistle blows, Luke picks up his saw and starts walking back toward the camp. "Where are you going?" Larry asks.*
>
> *"To sharpen my saw," Luke replies.*

In his bestseller *The Seven Habits of Highly Effective People*, Stephen Covey talks about the importance of keeping a sharp saw. He argues that making time to improve your skills is critical – especially if you're already overwhelmed with work.

This book is a tool to sharpen your fundraising saw.

As a fundraiser in today's world, you have three options available to you:

1. Keep doing the same thing and watch your results steadily worsen;

2. Work harder and harder and watch your results stay the same;

3. Work smarter and watch your results get better.

Which of these three options most turns your crank?

If you picked number 3, keep reading! If you picked number 1 or number 2, you might want to just go and turn on the TV. There might just be a Seinfeld rerun on right now.

"The definition of insanity is doing the same thing over and over again, but expecting a different result." – Albert Einstein

What safety net?

In the years following the Second World War, Canadians chose a different public policy path than our American neighbours.

We collectively built a social safety net – and more – to enhance our Canadian community. During the 1950s and 1960s, Canada implemented and expanded a host of public programs from old age and disability pensions, to Medicare, to postsecondary education and welfare. The public purse went even further, playing an active role in funding the arts and international development.

We as Canadians lived in a "generation of entitlement" until the late 1980s.

Then things changed. The Berlin Wall came down and the Soviet Union collapsed. The Cold War was over. Globalization was the new buzzword. The public debate was over free trade and the liberalization of commerce across national boundaries. Leaders like Ronald Regan, Margaret Thatcher and Brian Mulroney began articulating a different vision, one where the social safety net was a much less important part of the overall social and economic fabric.

The crunch hit the charitable sector hardest in the 1990s. During that decade, municipal, provincial and federal levels of government cut funding to our sector by some $15 billion.

At the same time, charitable giving in Canada was growing incrementally. Overall giving in Canada by 2004 was $8.9 billion, up from $4.5 billion in 1997. But this increase of $4.4 billion was nowhere close to filling the huge gap created by the government spending cuts of the previous decade.

The reaction of charities to government cuts was swift – and not always realistic. Boards and CEOs told their fundraisers to "get out there and raise more money".

The competition for donor dollars became fierce. Donors noticed the difference big-time. Their phones were now ringing off the hook. Their mailboxes were full to overflowing with appeals. Their doorbells kept ringing with volunteers (and now professionals) looking for donations.

Charities were desperate for cash. Donors were becoming overwhelmed.

Today we're still trying to find our equilibrium amid all the commotion and noise.

This chapter is brought to you by the letter S

In 1962 Everett Rogers wrote a book called *Diffusion of Innovations*. This book launched what is now commonly referred to as "S-curve theory". Rogers split the population into segments with respect to the quickness with which they adopt and use new innovations and technology. When plotted on a graph, these segments form a typical bell curve.

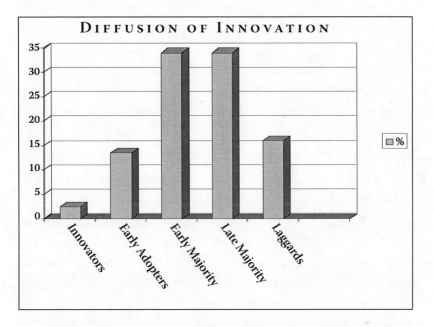

The innovators (2.5 per cent of the population) come first. They're the risk-takers – the bold explorers. Today, they're often geeks! Then come the early adopters (13.5 per cent). These are the social leaders. Their role is to make the innovation credible and acceptable. Following the lead of the early adopters, the early majority (34 per cent) bring the innovation in question into widespread use. Next, the late majority (34 per cent) join in because everyone else is doing it – and the perceived risk of adopting (the not-so-new) innovation is minimal. Lastly, the laggards (16 per cent) get into the innovation game. These are the people who were buying VHS videotape players when pretty much everyone else had progressed to DVDs!

Viral marketing gurus like Seth Godin (Unleashing the Idea Virus) and Malcolm Gladwell (*The Tipping Point*) still refer to these segments often in their writings.

The actual architecture of the S-curve was explained to us this way many years ago. The example used was the Big Three automakers (GM, Ford and Chrysler).

Henry Ford started mass-producing the Model T Ford in the early 20th century. Up to around the Great Depression, automobiles replaced the horse and buggy slowly. In fact, as with most innovations, auto producers lost money in their efforts to get the momentum ball rolling.

The Big Three automakers shot up their S-curve in the late forties, fifties and sixties. After the Second World War, car ownership became a symbol of middle class life, and families all over North America had a car or two. By the late 1960s, just about every household was driving – and they were all driving cars manufactured by the Big Three.

These cars were big! In fact, cars from the late sixties and early seventies were often nicknamed "boats" because of their immense size. In those days, size wasn't an issue because gasoline was plentiful and cheap.

The top of the S-curve for the Big Three was sudden and dramatic. On October 17, 1973, the Middle Eastern oil producing nations – with Saudi Arabia in the lead – announced that they would not sell oil to any countries that were supporting Israel in the Yom Kippur War against Egypt and Syria.

The price of gas in North America went through the roof.

The Big Three continued to build their "boats", assuming that high gas prices were just a momentary hiccup. Big mistake.

Out of nowhere came the Japanese with their Hondas, Toyotas and Datsuns. These cars were small, simple, cheap – and they were downright miserly when it came to gas consumption. The Honda Civic is still one of North America's most popular cars more than 30 years later.

When you reach the top of the S-curve you either ride out the decline (as the Big Three tried to do) or you create a new S-curve. In 1973 the Big Three had a near-monopoly on the North American automobile market. Today the market has fractured – and as you drive down the street you see cars, trucks and SUVs made in Japan, Germany, Sweden, Mexico and Korea and the Chinese are on their way!

The failure of the Big Three to recreate their S-curve in 1973 cost them half of the auto market. We estimate that those lost sales cost the North American automakers $1.8 billion in Canada alone in 2006.

If you stop and think about it, S-curves are all around us. Just think of recorded music. Vinyl albums gave way to cassettes. Cassettes gave way to CDs. CDs are giving way to MP3 players and digital downloading from the web.

We believe that S-curve theory applies to fundraising as well.

Many of the fundraising tactics we use today are at the top of their S-curves. We'll argue that direct mail, tele-fundraising, golf tournaments, lotteries and a host of other methods have maxed out and are about to decline.

Iceberg Philanthropy is all about using your direct mail program (which is probably at the top of its S-curve) and creating a new curve around bequests. Iceberg Philanthropy isn't brand new. It's more than an idea or a concept. Some non-profits began practicing Iceberg Philanthropy a couple of years ago.

The innovators have already started. It's time for the early adopters. The purpose of this book is to help launch the growth phase of that curve.

We predict that this particular curve has about a 20-year lifespan. The people who commit to Iceberg Philanthropy now will indeed take some risk. But they'll reap the greatest rewards. The people who wait (early and late majority) will get in later, with lower risk. But their returns will be lower as the marketplace becomes crowded.

The inherent challenge in this book is for you to identify yourself and your organization. Are you an early adopter? Early majority? Late majority? Or, perish the thought, a laggard?

You may in fact realize that you yourself are indeed an early innovator but the organization you're involved with is firmly planted in the late majority camp. If that's the case, we feel your pain.

Chapter Two
The old give and take

The four types of giving

We all give. To charities. To people in need.

We all want to help. We believe there are four categories of charitable giving. These four methods form a sort of food chain or ladder – with each step being more meaningful and committed than the one before.

Let's start at the bottom and work our way up.

Tippers

This is the "spare change" kind of gift you make with hardly any thought or consideration.

You're asked for something small and often you comply because it's just easier to say yes. You run your "instant cost-benefit analysis" through your head and decide that giving is the path of least resistance.

Here are a few examples of how you might tip:

* When you're downtown you give a toonie to the first homeless person who asks you for spare change. Call it your "karma insurance." You rationalize that the daily toonie is your insurance premium that will keep you from ending up on the street someday.

* Then there's the old "office chocolate bar sale." Someone at work has a kid whose school is on a fund-

raising drive. You get the e-mail from Sharon telling you that her kid's chocolate bars are at reception and they cost three bucks. You buy one so that Sharon won't think you're cheap.

◆ After supper, your doorbell rings. It's eight-year old Allison from two doors down. She's jumping rope for heart at school and asks if you'll sponsor her. You fill in the form on her clipboard and pull five bucks from your wallet.

Do you have a strong attachment to the homeless guy, the school or the issue of heart disease? Nope. Do you want to know how your donation is used? Not particularly. You simply want the transaction to be over with – to cross it off your mental to-do list.

Buyers

This is a combination of giving and receiving. You give some of your money. A portion of that money goes to the charity or the cause. But some of it comes back to you in the form of a benefit.

You might love to play golf. The charity golf tournament is a classic form of buying. For about a hundred bucks (sometimes a *lot* more) you get a round of golf at a great course, a good meal and a shot at some cool prizes.

Now you could play golf for less than a hundred bucks on your own, but the charity tournament lets you indulge in your passion for the game and to get the psychic reward of having done something good.

When you go to a special fundraising event, you're a buyer. It might be a gala dinner. A benefit concert. A wine auction. The list goes on and on.

All types of charitable gaming fit here as well. From 50-cent Nevada tickets to bingos to the big hospital mega-lotteries.

Buyers may or may not have much attachment to the charity sponsoring the event. They may or may not be loyal to the event. (Would you switch golf tournaments if a better offer came your way)?

Donors

As we move from buyer to donor, we're moving further up the ladder from self-interest to philanthropy.

We define the donor as someone who gives simply because she supports the mission and program of the charity – and wants to do her part to help.

The donor doesn't expect anything in return other than the satisfaction of doing a good deed. (Tax receipts have been shown not to be a significant motivator to give.)

Donors respond to direct mail appeals with $40 cheques. They make a $25 donation on their credit card when they're telemarketed. They may go online during a time of disaster and make a gift at a web site. They may decide to sponsor a child for $30 a month after watching a half hour infomercial on TV.

Donors usually give as an emotional impulse in response to an appeal. (We'll return to emotions later). The size of the gift is relatively small. You could make it without consulting your spouse or reviewing your household budget.

Donors by and large are more loyal (and more profitable in the long run) than tippers and buyers. They truly care about your work and want to help you succeed in your mission.

Investors

Ever heard the expression "give till it hurts"?

Investors are the next step up from donors. They make gifts that are more sacrificial. They are serious about making a difference. They're committed to your organization and your cause. They want to be partners and stakeholders – and not just supporters.

Major gift donors are investors. So are planned giving donors. Some monthly donors are investors too, depending on the amount of their monthly pledge.

The investor can't usually just make that investment on the spot. He or she needs to consider the gift. The investor often will consult with family or professional advisors. The investor may require a more specific proposal that outlines how the gift will be used by the charity and what outcomes can be expected.

A donor usually gives as an emotional impulse. The investor is also emotionally motivated but makes the investment gift rationally as well. The gift is considered carefully from a number of angles.

How do you give?

If you're like us, you probably give in all four ways. You tip the homeless guy and your neighbour's kid. You buy tickets to charity events that turn your crank. You probably make modest contributions to a number of charities and causes every year. You might also make one or two investment gifts to those organizations you're most connected to (perhaps those you also volunteer with).

Relating to the four types

As a fundraiser, you would obviously relate differently to tippers who give to your organization than you would to your investors. As we move up the giving food chain the expectations for communications, stewardship and a meaningful relationship increase.

You don't expect the homeless guy to send you a newsletter and tell you what he spent your toonie on. You don't expect Allison from down the street to send you a handwritten thank-you letter for your five-dollar pledge.

But if you've made a $50 per month commitment to a charity, your expectations are probably different. You want to feel that your involvement is paying dividends – and that your money is achieving something.

British fundraiser Ken Burnett first coined the phrase "relationship fundraising". Donors and investors by and large want to have a relationship with the charities they support. Tippers and buyers probably don't.

Taking stock of your portfolio

Take a look at your donor constituency from a portfolio perspective. Take the names on your database and break them out into the four categories of giving. What does your portfolio look like?

Generally speaking, the greater the percentage of contributors who fall into the donor and investor categories, the better off you are. Donors and investors have attached to you. They are more loyal. Future revenues from them are more predictable – and more profitable.

If a very high percentage of the people on your database are just buying lottery tickets and coming to golf tournaments, you might want to rethink your program and rebalance your portfolio.

This book is about helping you rebalance your portfolio. It's about helping you to maximize your investor potential from very ordinary donors.

The three types of asking

Just as there are four categories of giving, there are three fundamental ways in which we raise funds. Let's review them quickly now.

Selling

Our first experience at charitable fundraising came when we were about seven or eight years old.

One of us sold Cub apples in front of the grocery store, while the other went door-to-door with Girl Guide cookies. (We'll let you guess which did what).

We didn't pitch the cause. We didn't make our case for support. We didn't talk about how our lives were being moulded by our Cub or Guiding experience. We didn't articulate aspirations of being tomorrow's model citizens. We didn't talk about role models or building our characters.

We just asked people if they'd buy an apple or a box of cookies. And most of them did. The transaction was over. It usually took five or 10 seconds.

This is quick'n-dirty fundraising. Not much philanthropy involved. The emphasis on sales fundraising is the transaction – the now. The approach is straight up. "Please give me some money."

Selling is all too commonplace in the charitable sector today. Nevada tickets. Golf tournaments. Dinners and auctions. Sponsoring the neighbour's kid and buying that school-sponsored chocolate bar at the office.

In the world of fundraising relationships, this doesn't mean much to either party. It's quick. It's convenient. But it doesn't mean all that much.

Does selling raise a lot of money? Sometimes.

Just ask Scouts Canada. They raise millions of dollars selling popcorn every year. Our guess is that they did some market research and realized that popcorn was a more attractive offer than apples.

For most charities, selling is a necessary evil. The profit margin is low. It's a lot of work. It's not much fun. But it does generate some cash.

Marketing

We went to Wikipedia to find a nice digestible definition of marketing. Here's the one we liked best.

"The most widely accepted definition of marketing on a global scale comes from the Chartered Institute of Marketing (CIM) in the U.K. which is the largest marketing body in the world in terms of membership. The definition claims marketing to be the 'management process of anticipating, identifying and satisfying customer requirements profitably'. Thus, operative marketing involves the processes of market research, new product development, product life cycle management, pricing, channel management as well as promotion."

Marketing differs from selling in that it's much more strategic and, we think, a lot more fun. Prospects are selected with care. Messages are honed and crafted. Offers are carefully worded.

Perhaps the key difference between marketing and selling is that marketing meets a pre-existing need on the part of the customer, prospect or donor.

When that guy bought a Boy Scout apple or a box of Girl Guide cookies, the odds are that he hadn't been hankering for either to start off his day. When your neighbour's kid came to your door, you probably hadn't been wondering how you could do something to contribute to the cause of heart disease.

But if you've been watching TV news coverage of a tsunami in Asia – and if you have a history of giving to international aid organizations – the odds are you'd be very receptive if you received an emergency appeal from CARE Canada in your e-mail inbox. Or if your dad had just had successful triple bypass surgery at a local hospital, you might be looking to "pay them back" for his restored health and his renewed lease on life.

The art of marketing is reaching out to a large group of people at once – but reaching them as the individuals they are. By identifying common traits among groups of people, we're able to communicate to one. There can be true genius in this.

Today there are various media available to us as fundraising marketers. The mail still rules. But there's the phone, online appeals, direct response television (also known as DRTV), and advertising of all sorts.

Marketing is more efficient than selling. There is more front-end investment to be sure. But the payoff is richer. And the likelihood of a repeat donor is much greater than sales.

But don't take our word for it. Management consultant and author/guru Peter Drucker has this to say on the subject:

"The aim of marketing is to make selling superfluous. The aim of marketing is to understand the customer so well that the product or service fits him and sells itself." (Quoted from James Gregory Lord)

Relating

Now we come to the top of the fundraising pyramid. This is the very apex where we get to know those very top donors on a personal basis. We learn their likes and dislikes, their personal styles, their histories – even their hopes and dreams.

Recently we watched a colleague talk about her work on a local cable TV show. Susan Doyle is the President and CEO of the Ottawa Hospital Foundation. She's one of the best fundraisers we've ever met anywhere.

Susan was talking about her hospital's campaign and major gift fundraising. She talked at some length about the process. Cultivating the prospect. Really getting a fix on the donor's hopes and dreams. Finding common ground between the donor's aspirations and the goals of the hospital. Putting together the proposal that *sings* to the donor.

As we watched, we were struck not so much by Susan's words as by her face. She was simply glowing. As she talked about her donors, the joy just radiated from her eyes. Her smile was genuine and simply radiated her warmth. Her hand gestures gave her enthusiasm away.

Here was a professional woman who still shows a childlike joy for the work she does. No wonder she's the best. Enthusiasm and passion are infectious.

In his book *The Tipping Point*, viral marketing guru Malcolm Gladwell talks about the "sneezers" who spread the virus of new ideas. Great relationship fundraisers are great sneezers. They spread the virus of hope and passion and conviction and humanity.

Relationship fundraising has huge upsides.

It builds the greatest donor loyalty. It's the most profitable tactic of the three by far. It's also the most rewarding method of asking and giving for the fundraiser and the donor.

The only downside we can see is cost. Relationships are time-consuming. And in fundraising time is money.

Most charities don't have boards that volunteered so that they can be ambassadors and go spend their time in donors' living rooms. (Why do donors scare us so?).

Of course, the other option is simply to hire more fundraising staff – and direct them to build relationships with the top five per cent of your donor file. But relationships take time and the gratification isn't immediate

(We read recently that a major university expects an 18-month period to elapse between the first approach to a prospect and the realization of the gift).

So if your executive director or board will allow you to post five new major gift and planned giving positions this week, you probably don't need to read this book. If, on the other hand, you live in the real world with the rest of us, please read on.

Linking the asking to the giving

If you think about it, you'll quickly realize that the four types of giving and the three types of asking are usually connected to each other.

Asking type	Giving type
Selling	Tippers
Selling	Buyers
Marketing	Donors
Relating	Investors

Look again at your own fundraising portfolio. How have tippers given to you? What activities did you employ to generate those tips? Run through the chart and connect how your tactics match up with the way your donors have given to you.

We'll bet dollars to donuts that your fundraising program is a very close match to the table shown above.

When the homeless guy asks you for spare change, you're probably not inclined to include him as a beneficiary in your will. When you're asked for a three-year pledge at $1,000 a year, you're probably not inclined to say, "No thanks, but here's a toonie for your trouble."

Contrarian idea

This book is about taking an eraser to the matrix of conventional wisdom – rubbing out some lines and writing in some new ones.

You can generate investment gifts in a relationship strategic framework – by using marketing tactics. Put another way, you can create a new row in the fundraising matrix and make that matrix look like this.

Asking type	Giving type
Selling	Tippers
Selling	Buyers
Marketing	Donors
Marketing	**Investors**
Relating	Investors

This is the open space on the fundraising field. Using marketing tactics to generate investment gifts from donors simply isn't done much – at least not yet.

This is your opportunity to step out of that speeding parade and start a new parade of your own. Or at least to join a parade that is moving at a reasonable speed and doesn't have many floats.

Stay with us and we'll tell you how to get your parade started.

CHAPTER THREE
Where were you
on July 13, 1985?

Fraser's Live Aid story

I remember the Live Aid concert like it was yesterday. In fact, that amazing event took place more than 20 years ago.

July 13, 1985 was a beautiful sunny Saturday in Toronto. Normally I would have spent a lot of my day outside – but not this Saturday. I sat in my living room, glued to my TV, watching the first transatlantic rock concert of all time – beamed by satellite – all in aid of Ethiopian famine.

It was so cool!

Paul McCartney, Eric Clapton, Led Zeppelin, Dire Straits (with Sting), the Boomtown Rats, Bo Diddley, George Thorogood, The Who. Even David Bowie and Mick Jagger doing a duet of "Dancing in the Streets." And that was just part of the line-up at Wembley Stadium in England. There was a whole other concert at Veterans' Stadium in Philadelphia!

Phil Collins even performed at Wembley in the morning, jumped on a jet and performed in Philly that evening. Now that wouldn't make my teenage daughter sit up and take notice today– but it sure impressed the hell out of me in 1985!

During the broadcast, organizers ran ads asking viewers to call a 1-800 number and buy Live Aid T-shirts for $25 in support of the cause. I cracked out my (relatively new) MasterCard, called the number and put in my order.

Let's stop for a moment and go back to Chapter 2.

What was Live Aid doing with that ad? Were they selling? Marketing? Or Relating? How did they reach me?

What was I doing? Was I tipping, buying, giving or investing?

The first answer is a no-brainer. Live Aid was marketing to me – and marketing very well indeed. They knew me. They knew my likes and dislikes (at least musically). They knew how much to ask me for. And they knew I'd love the Africa map/guitar logo plastered across my chest. Smart job indeed.

The second answer is a bit more difficult. I'd have to say I was right on the borderline between buying and giving. I really wanted to support the fight against famine in Ethiopia. But, truth be told, I really wanted that T-shirt.

Would I have just called the number and made a $25 donation without the T-shirt in return? Probably.

But the T-shirt nailed it. It improved the likelihood of me picking up the phone from 60 per cent to 100 per cent. They closed me with that shirt.

The unfortunate thing about Live Aid is that they never followed up on their huge success. How many people (mostly Boomers who weren't into big-time charitable giving yet) gave or bought that day? What could have happened if the event turned into an ongoing cause? It could have been huge – and I might still be giving (probably $25 or $50 a month by now).

Alas, Bob Geldoff is a lead singer and not a fundraiser like you and us. Guess he didn't see the potential. Can't blame him for that.

Instead, Bob Geldoff returned in the summer of 2005 with the Live 8 concert. It just wasn't the same. I think I played golf that day. The TV glue was gone.

The consciousness of giving

Whether you're a fundraiser or not, ask yourself, "Why do people give?"

Most of us don't know the answer to this question as well as we should. We think the answer is found on two levels. The first more superficial level is that of the conscious, which raises two more questions: Why do people think they give? Why do they say they give?

This has been researched in some depth over the years. If you'll stick with us through a brief literature review, we'll then move on to what we think the real reasons are.

Perhaps our favourite answer is "because they're asked." As direct marketers, we were trained from the get-go that donors and prospects don't give if you don't ask. Not only that, the ask must be explicit (ask for a specific amount for a specific purpose – and ask for the gift now).

In fact, a former colleague in the consulting world, Betsy Clarke, used to run full-day fundraising seminars for junior fundraisers that were titled "A is for Ask." It's a good place to start with newbies.

Way back in the mid-nineties, we wrote our Certified Fund Raising Executive (CFRE) exams. In preparation, we read a number of fundraising "textbooks" written by some of the best and brightest fundraisers in the world. Here's a sampling of what they have to say.

James Greenfield (*Fundraising – Evaluating and Managing the Fund Development Process*) talks about the "sorting out" the donor runs through before making the gift decision:

◆   Is this charity legitimate?

◆   Why me?

◆   Why now?

◆   Why this much?

◆   Where will the money go?

◆   How local is this cause (matters more to some than others)?

◆   When will they ask again?

◆   Will my gift be acknowledged?

◆   Will the charity report to me on how my gift was used?

Joseph R. Mixer (*Principals of Professional Fundraising*) quotes a 1992 Gallup study of the reasons people give for their charitable giving. The Gallup hit parade (from top to bottom) reads like this?

1. The idea that "those with more should help those with less."

2. Being asked by a friend or associate.

3. Giving (and volunteering) causes a sense of personal satisfaction.

4. Giving is consistent with religious beliefs.

5. Giving back to the society that enabled them to prosper.

6. The cause or charity provides direct benefit to the donor or a loved one.

7. Setting an example to others.

8. Fulfilling a business or community obligation.

9. Creating a remembrance of oneself or a loved one.

10. Tax considerations.

11. Being encouraged to give by an employer.

Make a special note of the fact that tax considerations place next to last. We're going to come back and make an *über*rant about the planned giving sector and its obsession with this relatively unimportant matter!

Mixer also quotes U.S. studies that demonstrate the close correlation between both religious affiliation and volunteering and charitable giving. Our company's more recent quantitative research in Canada has found this link as well.

Harold J. (Si) Seymour (*Designs for Fundraising*) takes a different tack. He attributes giving to our social needs, namely:

- Humans share a responsible concern for their communities.

- Humans seek to be worthwhile members of worthwhile groups.

- Humans desire to be sought by other humans.

He combines these factors to coin the much-used phrase "pride of association."

In *The Raising of Money*, James Gregory Lord also has a social slant on his analysis of why people give. He argues simply and eloquently that people give to people. He writes, "People don't give to an institution. They give to the person who asks them. Often, a contribution is made because of how one person feels about another. The institutions may be almost incidental."

Lord also makes the case that "institutions have no needs" (We've always *loved* this idea). He makes the case that people give for people and not for things.

In other words (and these are our examples):

- We give to the sick and injured – more so than the hospital.

- We give to the students who need bursaries – more than the university.

- We give to the starving – more than the international development NGO.

◈ We give to the homeless – more than our local United Way.

Another great study of donor motivation is the book *The Seven Faces of Philanthropy* by Russ Alan Prince and Karen Maru File. They use a neat combination of segmentation and psychographics, which we like very much.

As direct marketers, we're naturally very familiar with segmentation. But in our case, segmentation usually revolves around the donor's previous giving behaviour. Let's use a direct mail donor example:

◈ How often has she given?

◈ When did she first give?

◈ When did she last give?

◈ Does she give at a particular time of year?

◈ How much does she usually give?

◈ How much did she give last time?

◈ Does she give to certain types of appeals (like direct mail appeals containing a premium like address labels) and not to others (appeals with no premium)?

◈ Does she have particular giving characteristics (like giving on her credit card, or being very phone-, as well as mail-responsive)?

Direct marketers often use the "RFM" (for recency-frequency-monetary value) approach to data segmentation – all in the interest of creating greater efficiency in a direct marketing program.

The authors of *Seven Faces* bring a segmentation approach to major gift donors and prospects. But rather than segmenting on previous behaviours, they segment on the donor's values, thoughts and beliefs. It's cool stuff indeed.

In this book, major gift donors are split into (not surprisingly) seven "psychographic clusters" – each with its own way of seeing one's self and the world around us.

Here is a scan (in our words) of the seven types outlined in the book:

1. *The Communitarian:* This group believes that "it takes a village to raise a child." Communitarians believe that we need each other to survive and thrive. They believe we need to reject the "rugged individualist cowboy" mentality we tend to see from the political neo-conservative right.

2. *The Devout:* These folks are very much motivated to give by religious and spiritual values and teachings. Simply put, they believe that it's divine will that we be charitable.

3. *The Investor:* These are the donors who see the business advantages of giving. They're the ones who would see the tax benefits of making a gift of securities or who might anticipate that a new community pool would mean less graffiti on his storefront.

4. *The Socialite:* These donors enjoy the experience or the "event" of giving. Giving is an opportunity to have fun with friends and do good at the same time. Look at the community page of your local paper and see the pictures of the people who attended the charity gala. Voilà.

5. *The Altruist:* These are the people who give from a moral (as opposed to religious) imperative. They give because "giving is the right thing to do." The altruist's reward is the psychic gratification of doing good deeds. She does not want her name on your donor recognition wall or to have her name listed in your annual report.

6. *The Repayer:* This is your classic donor who "wants to give something back." Often this donor is now successful but faced challenges earlier in life and was helped by someone along the way. The classic repayer might be a university alumnus who received bursaries in his undergrad days. Now that he's a millionaire, he wants to help a young person who's struggling to pay tuition. One client of ours is CARE Canada. There are still CARE donors who give because they want to repay for the CARE package they receive in post-Second World War Europe.

7. *The Dynast:* These donors typically come from "old money" and were brought up to believe that giving is expected of them as part of family membership. These are the people who inherited – rather than created – wealth. Giving helps build and maintain the family brand.

In their book *Building Donor Loyalty*, U.K. authors Adrian Sargeant and Elaine Jay devote an entire chapter to "Understanding Giving Behaviour." Here they outline their five key motivators for charitable giving. Those motivators are:

1. *Self-interest:* The idea here is that the donor receives something in return for his gift. Their definition of self-interest is broad enough to include improvements in the donor's material, emotional and/or spiritual well-being. The wide range of *rewards* for giving (under this broad umbrella) include:

    ◆ increase in self-esteem

    ◆ atonement for "sins"

    ◆ recognition

    ◆ access to services or programs provided by the charity

    ◆ reciprocation

    ◆ honouring or memorializing loved ones

    ◆ tax benefits.

2. *Sympathy:* In this case the donor is emotionally moved by the plight of a fellow human being. She feels that the suffering in question is "inappropriate" and wishes to provide relief from that suffering.

3. *Empathy:* Empathy and sympathy are not the same. Empathy is when the donor's emotions are aroused by the emotional expression of another. So a donor might feel sympathy for a child with cystic fibrosis and feel empathy for that child's mother who wrote the fundraising letter on behalf of the Canadian Cystic Fibrosis Foundation. The authors note that it's important not to "overdo" empathy, since too much emotional charge can distress the donor to the point of inaction (namely, no gift).

4. *Belief in social justice:* As the category name implies, these donors place a high value on the idea of justice, equity and fairness. When they see injustice, inequity and unfairness, they are motivated to give to right the wrong.

5. *Desire to follow social norms:* This behaviour is driven by the donor *seeing others doing it.* Springing from a desire to belong, these donors will give in order to be accepted and normal members of their tribe.

Back to Fraser and Live Aid

As I reread all this material, I tried to get a *conscious* handle on why I sent my $25 to the Live Aid Foundation back in 1985:

◈ My friend Betsy says that "A is for Ask". Right on. If I hadn't been asked to call that number with my MasterCard handy, I wouldn't have picked up the phone in the first place.

❖ Did I "sort out" the gift as Greenfield has outlined? Not really. Starving people in Ethiopia was pretty much the extent of it.

❖ If we go back to the Gallup list outlined by Mixer, I'd say the top three items on the hit parade would describe me. I believed then (as I do now) that we should help our less fortunate brothers and sisters. I was asked by someone important (the lead singer of the Boomtown Rats no less). And it felt great to hang up that phone and go back to the telecast, feeling like I'd become a part of it all.

❖ Lord's "social" reasons certainly came into play. I certainly didn't give to an institution. Indeed, I didn't know at the time what the Live Aid Foundation even was. I gave because I couldn't ignore the suffering of hungry human beings. I also gave because one of my favourite rock stars asked me. I probably wouldn't have responded if Doris Day had done the pitch.

❖ I gave as two of the seven faces of philanthropy. The communitarian in me included Ethiopians as my global neighbours. And the little altruistic voice inside me (my conscience) simply ordered me to do something. On July 13, 1985, passivity on my part simply wasn't an acceptable option.

❖ Finally, Adrian Sargeant and Elaine Jay really nailed me with their five motivators for giving. I gave out of self-interest. In my case the feeling that I was "a part of" a magical day I'd remember for the rest of my life. Obviously I sympathized with the famine victims in

Ethiopia, but I also empathized with the passion of the performers who donated their time and talent to bring Live Aid to life. Did I give according to some social norm directive? I'd like to think not but, if that's the case, why did I want that T-shirt so badly (I think I'm busted on this one)? Last but not least, social justice is one of the true passions in my life. A no-brainer here.

Memo to Bob Geldoff

Oh yeah, one more thing. I never did get my T-shirt.

So, if you run into Sir Bob on the street in London or Belfast, would you ask him to put one in the mail? I'd still love to have that guitar and map of Africa on my chest some day.

But is this the definitive answer?

This chapter has presented a (perhaps too cursory) review of the conventional wisdom within the fundraising community about why donors and prospects give to charities and causes. It's the rationale for giving. The explanation. The mindful articulation.

But is it the whole story behind donor motivation? We're convinced it isn't.

In the next chapter, we'll do our level best to convince you that there's much more to this story than meets the eye, or the books-for-sale table at a conference of the Association of Fundraising Professionals or the Canadian Association of Gift Planners.

Chapter Four
Subconscious giving – emotion and impulse

Most fundraising literature we've read deals very much with the conscious mind. Prospects and donors make conscious decisions. They analyze, consider options, think, decide and then they act.

But how do they feel when they give? We're by no means psychologists, but we believe there's much more to giving than conscious decisions and conscious acts. In this chapter we hope to convince you we're right.

Life's defining moments

We'd like you to do a little exercise for us right now.

Close your eyes, centre yourself and take a few long slow deep breaths. Once you've dumped most of the here-and-now from your mind, go back to one or two of the most important moments of your life. Not years, or weeks or days. Moments.

Go to that moment and relive it as best you can. Experience it fully and completely. Don't work hard at doing this. Just let yourself go to that moment and be there as totally as you can.

Fraser's moments

There were two such moments in my life.

One was at 11:50 p.m., October 19, 1988. I was in a birthing room at Women's College Hospital in Toronto.

There were six of us altogether. My wife Nanci had just delivered our child. Her mother was there, being very quiet and unobtrusive. Our doctor, Elaine, and our nurse, Jennifer, were busy doing what doctors and nurses do in the moments after a delivery.

I was standing at Nanci's right hip – totally stunned and awed. Before I knew it, Jennifer handed my baby to me wrapped in a blanket. I gingerly held her in my arms and whispered, "Hi, pumpkin" (I'm starting to cry as I write this). She gazed up into my eyes with this expression of "knowing." Her look seemed focused. She seemed to be saying, "There you are. I know you."

I had two overwhelming emotions in that moment.

The first was total awe at the miracle that was happening before my eyes. I had actually been a part of creating a new human life. Me! How in the world was that possible? It was overwhelming and wonderful – and the most loving moment I've ever known.

The second emotion was tremendous protectiveness. This overwhelming instinct just got into my face and demanded that I sacrifice whatever it might take to keep this new life safe and secure.

That child was my life's masterpiece. She was then – and she is today.

The second was 6:20 p.m. June 21, 1999.

Again the moment took place in a hospital. But this time it was in the Intensive Care Unit at the General Campus of the Ottawa Hospital.

My dad, brother, sisters, brothers-in-law, a cousin and I were gathered around the bed in a very dimly lit room. The only sound was that high-pitched beep beep of a pulse monitor.

My mom lay in that bed – dying. She had been very sick for a while – and now her time had come.

The sound of the monitor suddenly went from "beep, beep, beep" to "mmmmmmmmmm" – and she was gone from us. Gone from me. Forever.

Again I was overwhelmed by emotion.

The first feeling was empathy. She had been so debilitated near the end. This woman who possessed such energy, enthusiasm, intelligence and warmth all her life had been stripped down to this pale body with lifeless eyes. From such strength to such weakness.

It hurt me so much to see her in pain – and so helpless. It just wasn't her. She didn't deserve it.

The second emotion in that moment was fear.

My mom had been my hero and my role model. She had taught me so much by her example. How to engage people and make them feel good about themselves. How to sort through problems and find strategic answers. How to be curious about life and the world. How to laugh and touch and be open to the love of others. (Now, I'm crying again).

In that moment I simply had no idea what I was going to do without her – even though I was a 44-year-old grown-up man with a child of my own. But, in truth, I wasn't a grown man at all in that moment. I was a very scared little boy whose mom was gone and not coming back.

I often ask workshop and seminar participants to take a few minutes and do the "defining moments" exercise. Then I ask volunteers to share their stories. Someone always makes me cry.

A first kiss. A breast cancer diagnosis. Losing a child. A marriage proposal. Often, like mine, their moments involve birth and death too.

Then I ask them, "When you were in that moment, were you thinking or feeling?" No one ever says, "Thinking." And I'll bet you're no different.

Nice stories, but what's the point?

The point is simply this. We humans are – at our very core – primitive, instinctual, emotional creatures. We act primarily on impulse, an impulse that's generated in a very tiny part of our brains.

Most of our behaviours and decisions are not made consciously. They are made in the subconscious. The conscious mind can explain and rationalize our decisions and behaviours but it didn't cause them to happen.

The previous chapter provided a cursory review of the conventional wisdom within the fundraising community about what we call "conscious giving." This chapter – one that we feel passionate about – deals with the still largely unexplored and unexplained domain of subconscious giving.

Let's start with God

In his book *New Revelations – A Conversation With God*, Neale Donald Walsch writes of an ordinary man who asks a question to God. Totally unexpectedly (to the man that is), God answers – and a six-hour conversation ensues.

During that conversation, God states, "All human action and all human response is triggered by either love or fear – and most often it is fear."

That simple statement stayed with us. We truly believe that we are that simple in our anthropology and neurology.

In another part of the same book God states, "Humankind behaves in accordance with its beliefs. To change behaviours, it is necessary to first change belief."

That one resonated with us too – big-time.

Okay, enough new age spirituality. Let's move on to more solid science.

Ego states

Sigmund Freud is world-renowned as the father of psychoanalysis. His work has been tremendously influential in the popular imagination – popularizing such notions as the unconscious, defence mechanisms, Freudian slips, and dream symbolism.

Freud introduced the idea of the three components of personality: the id, ego and super ego.

Later, in the 1950s and 1960s, Eric Berne adapted Freud's thinking into the approach called Transactional Analysis (or TA). Berne defined three ego states: the Child, Adult and Parent. He argues that we are in one of these states at any given moment in time and that our behaviour and actions are very much driven by the state we are in:

- Our Child is emotional, playful, sensual and not terribly rational. Our Child feels.

- Our Adult is our mental computer. In this state, we gather empirical information and make rational and thoughtful decisions.

- Our Parent is the rule-maker and rule-obeyer. For example, Parent language often contains words like "always," "must," "should" and "never."

Let's look at three gift examples and the ego state that drives them. These gifts are all made by Marie. She's a 72-year-old widow who has just sold her husband's company. She wants to give some of her newly acquired wealth to good causes:

- Marie sits in her living room with a representative from Girl Guides Canada. As they sip tea, Marie regales her new friend with stories and memories from her days as a girl at summer camp in the 1940s. On impulse, she runs upstairs and comes back with a photo album with pictures of her and her girlfriends at the campfire, at the beach and in canoes. Marie decides to put Girl Guides into her will.

- Later that same day, Marie meets with a representative of the United Way at their offices. She's dressed in a tailored suit and she's carrying a folder containing research she's done about various United Wayfunded agencies. Marie wants to make a community investment in youth programs. She wants to keep troubled teens off the street, help them go on to college, cut down on the graffiti downtown and help people her age feel safer in their neighbourhoods. Marie has asked for the meeting because she wants to negotiate what type of gift – and to which agency – would best achieve her objectives.

◆ The next day Marie meets with her church pastor and the chair of her congregation's finance committee. During their meeting Marie emphasizes how she feels a duty to give to the church, that her parents had "raised her right," that tithing to the church is a moral obligation to anyone who truly shares the faith.

Can you see the three ego states at play? Marie is in her Child state when she gives to the Girl Guides. She's in her Adult state when she gives to the United Way. And, she's in her Parent state when she gives to her church.

Ego states matter in fundraising. Your approach – whether in a face-to-face meeting or in direct mail copy – will be best received if it *matches* the ego state the donor is in when the approach is made.

What state is the donor in when she decides whether to make the gift or not? Figure this out (and it's not that hard) and you're going to score way more gifts.

By the way, 99 per cent of the time, the donor is going to have no idea what state she's in. We're not suggesting that you manipulate this knowledge in an unethical way. But if you can tune in, you'll relate much more successfully.

In his best-selling book *I'm OK – You're OK*, Thomas A. Harris, M.D. explains the baby's need for stroking and how we live for strokes for the rest of our lives. Fascinating stuff indeed. Learn to give great strokes – and to receive them appropriately – and you'll be a much more effective fundraiser (and human being for that matter).

The ammig — what?

Every fundraiser should become acquainted with the amygdala (pronounced ah-MIG-dah-lah).

It's the walnut-sized part of our brain located at its base, near the top of the spinal column. The amygdala is the brain we started out with thousands and thousands of years ago. It's also commonly called the old brain, the snake brain, or the reptilian brain.

According to Wikipedia, the amygdala is "the region of the brain, located in the medial temporal lobe, believed to play a key role in the emotions, such as fear and pleasure, in animals and humans."

Let's take a stab at this. The amygdala is the part of the brain that drives our instinct for survival. We are still genetically programmed to be on the lookout for predators. When a predator comes near, we don't have a lot of time to ask, "How hungry does he look?" We need to either fight or run (or, in the case of rabbits, simply surrender and offer up our neck so we can get it over with!). The amygdala drives our need to survive. It rules the rest of the brain. And yet we're totally unaware of it. In fact, most of us have probably never even heard of it.

If you watch the Simpsons on TV (which Fraser can't help doing with great regularity), you'll be familiar with

Homer's unthinking reaction to the smell of a juicy steak on Ned Flanders' barbecue, or a billboard promoting Duff beer. Homer's brain didn't really evolve much past the amygdala.

In his book *Emotional Intelligence,* Daniel Goleman describes research conducted by a neuroscientist named Joseph LeDoux. This research discovered neurons in the brain that serve as "back alleys" that shortcut or bypass the neocortex area of the brain. In other words, in certain situations your amygdala will drive a response in milliseconds – before the thinking part of your brain has even begun to process the decision.

Goleman offers this example:

"While the hippocampus remembers the dry facts, the amygdala retains the emotional flavour that goes with those facts. If we try to pass a car on a narrow two-lane highway and narrowly miss having a head on collision, the hippocampus retains the specifics of the incident, like what stretch of road we were on, who was with us and what the other car looked like. But it is the amygdala that ever after will send a surge of anxiety through us whenever we try to pass in similar circumstances."

To quote LeDoux, "The hippocampus is crucial in recognizing a face as that of your cousin. But it is the amygdala that adds you don't really like her."

So where does this rubber hit the road?

We know. We know.

This has been all theoretical gobbledygook so far. Thanks for staying with it. Now let's put it to use.

In Chapter 3 we reviewed some fundraising literature by authors you're most likely familiar with. Now we'd like to take you out of the realm of fundraising literature and into the world of psychology, sales and marketing. We're convinced that there's knowledge here you can put to good use. In fact, let's start with an author you may well be familiar with to get you started.

Thin slicing

In his best-selling book *Blink*, Malcolm Gladwell makes a powerful case for how dominant the instinctive and unconscious mind is in our decision-making. He argues that the study of the "adaptive unconscious" is one of the most important fields of study in psychology today. We believe he's right.

We've all heard the expression that you only get one chance to make a first impression. Here's Gladwell's proof of that in his own words:

"How long, for example, did it take you, when you were in college, to decide how good a teacher your professor was? A class? Two classes? A semester? The psychologist Nalini Ambady once gave students three ten-second videotapes of a teacher – with the sound turned off – and found they had no difficulty at all coming up with a rating of the teacher's effectiveness. Then Ambady cut the clips back to five seconds, and the ratings were the same. They were remarkably consistent even when she showed the students just two seconds of videotape. Then Ambady compared those snap judgments of teacher effectiveness with evaluations of those same professors made by their students after a full semester of classes, and *found that they were essentially the same* (our emphasis)."

Picture yourself with that two-second video clip. How much conscious calculating, thinking and assessing can you do? Not much.

The old brain

French authors Patrick Renvoise and Christopher Morin wrote a fascinating book called *Selling to the Old Brain*.

We're all no doubt familiar with the left and right hemispheres of the brain. The left hemisphere is linear and logical. The right hemisphere is conceptual and creative.

Renvoise and Morin argue that neuroscience has made a more detailed segmentation of the brain possible, one that is more instructive in understanding the human decision-making process. As fundraisers, we're all about influencing human decisions, *n'est-ce pas*?

They describe the human brain as having three distinct, but connected, components:

- The new brain is the thinking, analytical computer in our head. It processes information rationally.

- The middle brain drives our emotions and gut feelings.

- The old brain listens (sometimes) to the other two brains. But it runs the show. The old brain, which contains the amygdala, makes the decisions.

The authors make a compelling case that in order to market a product or service (or charitable cause, we'd suggest) effectively, you must speak directly to the old brain.

"Most of us buy emotionally and then justify our decisions rationally. And most of us do business with people we like. Neither of these factors is adequately addressed in traditional 'rational' sales and marketing approaches because they aren't necessarily rational or logical."

If you're interested in learning more about the importance of being liked by your donors and prospects, read *Love is the Killer App* and *The Likeability Factor* by Tim Sanders. You can actually learn a disciplined system to become more likeable!

But back to our French authors. They argue that only six types of stimuli speak directly to the old brain:

◆ It's all about me. It's critical to speak directly to the donor's self-interest or she'll tune you out. One of our first direct mail copywriting lessons was to count the number of times we'd written the word "you" in the letter.

◆ Use contrast. The old brain relates contrasts like before and after, with and without, big and small.

◆ Be tangible. Phrases like "software solutions for the non-profit sector" don't register because they're too vague. Pizza Pizza hit the nail on the head when it began offering "30 minutes or it's free."

◆ The beginning and the end will be remembered. The middle will be forgotten. Keep this in mind when you're writing your next fundraising letter or preparing for your next major gift ask.

◈ Use visuals. The old brain relies on visual images because the optical nerve is 25 times faster than the auditory nerve. Maybe that's how our Neanderthal ancestors survived those sabre toothed tiger attacks.

◈ Appeal to emotions. Emotional experiences release chemicals within the brain that help us memorize information. Direct mail copywriters know this. Most planned giving officers we've met don't.

Influence Voodoo

In his book *Influence – the Psychology of Persuasion,* Robert B. Caldiani outlines the "six weapons of influence" that can be used proactively to influence the decision-making and behaviour of others. Here's a quick and dirty summary of those six weapons:

1. Reciprocity. People have an innate need to repay acts of kindness or generosity. Caldiani quotes a cool experiment where a researcher sent Christmas cards to complete strangers. A staggering number of those strangers returned the favour by sending him a card the following Christmas – without any question as to who he was!

2. Consistency and commitment. People place a high value on predictability – both their own and that of others. That's why the neighbour on the beach is much more likely to stop a thief if you'd

asked her to watch your stuff before you went for a swim. This one's all about walking the walk – and not just talking the talk.

3. Social proof. People are definitely more likely to do something if they see others doing it too. (This harkens back to the lemmings we talked about earlier). Research has shown that canned laughter in TV sitcoms actually causes us to laugh more than if the Seinfeld episode in question had no canned laughter. Really. That's one reason why we're such fans of using testimonials in many forms of fundraising. They provide social proof.

4. Liking. This one's simple. We're more likely to comply with a request from someone we like than someone we don't like – or someone we're indifferent to. So, in selecting your solicitors and messengers, it's important to make sure that they have lots of what Tim Sanders calls "the likeability factor."

5. Authority. People will follow the lead or the direction of people in positions of authority who they respect. Not long ago, we watched the documentary movie "An Inconvenient Truth" which features former U.S. Vice President Al Gore doing PowerPoint presentations on global warming. There's no question that we *bought* the movies message in large part because we consider Gore to be a credible messenger.

6. Scarcity. We place a higher value on things that we believe are scarce. Scarcity creates urgency to act. To buy. To give. Ever watch the Shopping Channel on TV? They always have this count-down clock in the corner of the screen remind-ing you that you only have 17 minutes and 23 seconds to act on this terrific offer. To us, this is the toughest *weapon of influence* to use in chari-table fundraising. The example that comes to mind are those "dream of a lifetime" lotteries run by big hospitals and health charities, in which the deadline for the early bird draw is this Friday.

Your local bookstore or websites like amazon.com no doubt have dozens of titles on the subject of influence. Most are written from a business-sales-marketing per-spective. But they contain information and approaches that can easily be adapted by fundraisers.

Kurt W. Mortensen, in his book *Maximum Influence*, lists what he calls the 12 laws of power persuasion. They are dissonance, obligation, connectivity, social validation, scarcity, verbal packaging, contrast, expecta-tions, involvement, esteem, association and balance.

We won't bore you with descriptions of all 12 laws because they repeat material we've already covered. We'll just mention one briefly – the law of connectivity.

People like donors and prospects will respond favour-ably to – and are more likely to comply with the wishes of – people they feel a connection with. That connection is driven by four factors:

- *Attractiveness*. People assume that attractive people are kind, intelligent and trustworthy.

- *Similarity*. We gravitate toward, and connect with, other people in whom we see similar opinions, personality traits, backgrounds or lifestyles.

- *People skills*. We also connect with people who are good at connecting with us. Mortensen quotes a Harvard University study that found that twice as many employees were fired for their failure to get along with others as were fired for failure to do their work. He also quotes a study by the Carnegie Institute of Technology that found that 85 per cent of management success was driven by people skills – and only 15 per cent was driven by technical knowledge.

- *Rapport*. This is that instant feeling of connection that is driven in chief by body language and by mirroring and matching.

It bears repeating that we are perceived by others as follows:

- 55 per cent visual (our body language)

- 38 per cent vocal (the tone of our voice)

- 7 per cent verbal (what we actually say).

In his book *The Science of Influence*, Kevin Hogan repeats many of the principles we've already talked about. He does, however, talk compellingly about first impressions:

"Your body language and your physical appearance will jump-start your instant likeability, your persuasiveness, and most importantly how you are perceived by every person who meets you. You have less than ten seconds and realistically closer to four seconds to make a good first impression on those with whom you come into contact. A world of research clearly indicates that you will be judged professionally and personally in the first few seconds of your meeting someone for the first time. In fact, your first impression is recorded and is used as a yardstick for all future communication by those you meet. Whatever that first impression is going to be on your part, you want it to be intentional and on purpose."

Which takes us nicely back to Malcolm Gladwell's *Blink* and the idea of thin slicing, where we started this chapter.

It's not our intention to give you a psychology seminar here. Rather, we believe it's critical that those of us who fundraise have a deeper appreciation of how our donors really behave – and how emotional and instinctive triggers drive our decisions and behaviours in ways we don't consciously understand.

A little further on, we'll bring some of these laws and principles into play as we describe what Iceberg Philanthropy is and how it works. Stay with us. It'll be worth it!

Chapter Five

The "ordinary" donor below the waterline

Meet Jacqueline

Jacqueline Murphy was born just before Christmas in 1935. One of six children, Jacqueline grew up on a farm just outside Weyburn, Saskatchewan with her parents and five brothers and sisters.

The family didn't have much when Jacqueline was growing up. The Depression turned into the rationing of the Second World War. The family worked hard for very little money. Yet compared to many others, they fared well.

Jacqueline was a good, if not exceptional, student. She was a member of her local 4-H Club and the family attended St. James Anglican Church in Weyburn where her dad was an elder.

When Jacqueline finished high school, she enrolled in business college in Regina. At 19, she started her first secretarial job with an insurance company.

A year later she met a young history teacher named Walter Parisiuk at a church dance. He began courting her and they married in 1956.

Three children soon followed and Jacqueline stayed home with the children until 1976. When her youngest was in Grade 12, Jacqueline at age 41 took the leap back into the workforce and found a job as an administrative assistant to an insurance broker in Regina. She stayed in that job until she retired in 2000. Walter had retired two years earlier.

Today Jacqueline and Walter live an orderly and busy life. Walter is an avid golfer and curler. Jacqueline volunteers at her local hospital and is very involved in her church. She is also the past-president of the Regina Bridge Club. Jacqueline and Walter spend their summers at their cottage near Prince Albert. Their children, now in their fifties, make the annual pilgrimage there with their spouses and children.

Their lifestyle is modest. They live on a household income of about $58,000 a year, which is quite enough since the house is long-since paid for and they have no debt.

In addition to her volunteer work, Jacqueline gives donations regularly to a number of local and national charities. She believes deeply in the Golden Rule and believes it's her duty to give to those who are less fortunate than herself. She and Walter support 10 to 12 charitable causes each year with modest gifts of usually between \$30 and \$50.

Jacqueline grew up before the advent of television and is very comfortable with print media. She spends at least an hour with her newspaper every day and prefers to receive charitable appeals and make donations through the mail. She's most comfortable reading charitable fund-raising letters at her kitchen table where she doesn't feel the pressure of telephone calls or canvassers at the door.

About 10 years ago, Jacqueline began to feel over-whelmed by the growing number of appeals she was receiving – all from apparently worthy causes. At first she felt guilty because she simply didn't have the money to support them all. Then she became irritated because she felt these charities were just being greedy and unrealistic in their requests. Lately Jacqueline has been thinking about narrowing the list of charities she supports by making somewhat larger gifts to those organizations (like the local hospital and a national breast cancer research organization) where she wants to have the most impact.

Six months ago Jacqueline and Walter did a com-prehensive review of their financial situation. They were amazed to learn that their house and cottage combined were valued at close to \$500,000.

Jacqueline's two older sisters passed away last year, and Jacqueline has been thinking about updating her will. Her three children are all professionally successful and financially independent. Her five grandchildren — whose ages range between 17 and 24 — are just starting out in life. Three are still in university and two are just starting careers and marriages.

Jacqueline is planning to talk to Walter about leaving $65,000 to each grandchild and giving the rest to her church, her hospital and the breast cancer organization she cares so much about. She likes the idea of leaving a personal legacy to her family, to her faith, to her community and to the fight against a disease that took the lives of her mother, aunt and sister.

Jacqueline has reached a point in her journey where she accepts that death is simply a part of life. She approaches her own mortality practically and wants to end her life the way she's lived it – committed to her family, her community and her church.

So why does Jacqueline matter?

Jacqueline is typical of those donors who send your organization $35 cheques through the mail. She's the classic *ordinary* donor who occupies a place in your iceberg (or pyramid) far below the waterline.

Your major gift officer pays no attention to donors like Jacqueline. Nor does your planned giving officer. Jacqueline is ordinary. She's been beneath your radar for years. Yet she might well have been giving to you consistently for 10 or 20 years.

This book is all about Jacqueline – and the hundreds of thousands of donors like her who are giving to Canadian charities today.

Understanding Jacqueline is one of the keys to understanding the tremendous potential of Iceberg Philanthropy. Connecting meaningfully with Jacqueline is the key to leveraging the potential revenue that Iceberg

Philanthropy could make available to you and your cause.

Let's look at the hard data

When we were starting out at charitable fundraising almost 20 years ago, the late Fran Lowe used to encourage us to write direct mail fundraising letters to "an elderly aunt." At the time, we took her at her word – and the approach worked.

Many years later, we felt we needed more solid data. The market had become much more competitive, as we've already discussed, and we wanted to have the clearest possible picture of who exactly gave donations through the mail. Specifically, we wanted to know:

- What are their demographic characteristics?

- How do they give?

- How frequently do they give?

- Who are they giving to?

- Are they capable of giving more?

We went looking for quantifiable data that could help us answer these questions. And we didn't find it.

Despite the fact that direct mail fundraising had been around for decades – and was generating hundreds of millions of dollars a year in Canada – no one had ever done a quantitative research study specifically targeted at donors who give primarily through the mail.

We decided we needed to be the first.

In 2003 our consulting firm, FLA Group, partnered with Mal Warwick and Associates of Berkeley, California and conducted the first ever statistically valid research study of North American direct mail donors.

While our research looked at both American and Canadian donors, we'll keep our focus north of the border for the purposes of this book.

Here's what we did:

- We gathered donor records from a wide array of Canadian non-profits, most of whom had charitable status. We asked for donors who had given two or more gifts through the mail in the past three years. We also excluded monthly donors, donors who had made gifts of $500 or more and donors who had been flagged for planned giving purposes in any way. We wanted to interview the ordinary donor – the donor like Jacqueline – who sends the $35 cheque with no muss no fuss.

- We partnered with Jim Matsui of Lang Research to oversee the actual survey work, provide professional editorial support to our questionnaire and help us interpret the results.

- We designed a questionnaire of some 58 questions on a wide variety of topics.

- The research was conducted entirely in English.

- Five hundred interviews were completed by telephone with the donors described above during the first week of March 2003. The average interview took 13½ minutes to complete.

♦ Results of this survey are considered accurate plus or minus 4.4 per cent, 19 times out of 20.

Here's what we found.

Jacqueline is very real

First and foremost, we wanted to know as precisely as possible who these direct mail donors really are. Here's what we found:

♦ 70 per cent of direct mail donors are over the age of 65 and 83 per cent are over the age of 55. These donors belong to the Civic generation that was born before or during the Second World War. Only six per cent of donors surveyed were under the age of 45.

♦ Female direct mail donors outnumber males by a factor of two to one.

♦ 70 per cent of the donors surveyed were retired. Only 15 per cent were still working full-time. The remainder described themselves as being part-time workers or homemakers.

♦ Direct mail donors are pretty evenly split when it comes to education attained. About half had finished their education at high school or college while half had attended university.

♦ Over half of direct mail donors reported household incomes between $25,000 and $75,000. Only 14 per cent of the donors we surveyed had household incomes in excess of $75,000.

◆ Marital status was an even split. Exactly half of the donors surveyed were married while half were not. The not-married group included widowed, separated/divorced and never married.

◆ Direct mail donors are empty-nesters – 82 per cent reported having no dependent children.

◆ Three out of five direct mail donors attend religious services on a regular (41 per cent) or occasional (18 per cent) basis. This rate of church attendance is almost three times the national average.

◆ Only three ethnic groups showed up significantly in our survey. Donors responded as being of British origin (59 per cent), other European (16 per cent) and Canadian (11 per cent), even though we didn't offer Canadian as an "ethnic choice." Three per cent reported French heritage. No other group made up more than one per cent of the survey respondent population.

Based on these findings, we're convinced that Jacqueline is a very accurate composite of today's typical direct mail donor. Why, we've even googled a photo on the web and named it Jacqueline! If you'd like a copy of her picture, just email fgreen@theflagroupinc.com.

How much does Jacqueline give?

In our survey, we asked direct mail donors how much they give annually to charities. Here's how they responded (note: the totals that follow represent the total of all donations given by a donor to all charities over the course of a year).

- ◆ The largest group (40 per cent of those surveyed) said they give between $200 and $1,000 to charity each year.

- ◆ 28 per cent reported giving between $1,000 and $5,000 annually.

- ◆ 12 per cent said they gave more than $5,000 to charity annually.

- ◆ Only eight per cent reported giving less than $200.

So if Jacqueline is the average donor, she probably makes charitable donations to the tune of $500 to $1,000 per year. That's pretty generous considering her modest household income!

By the way, over a third (37 per cent) of the donors we surveyed reported making single gifts of $500 or more to a single charity.

Who does Jacqueline give to?

First off, we asked direct mail donors how many charitable causes they'd given donations to in the past 12 months:

- ◆ Nine per cent of donors surveyed said they donated to five or fewer charities.

- ◆ The largest single group (44 per cent) gave to between six and 10 charities.

- 12 per cent said they'd given to between 11 and 19 charities.

- More than one in three (35 per cent) donors surveyed reported making donations to more than 20 charities in the past year!

Next, we asked what types of charities and causes donors had made gifts to in the past 12 months. Keep in mind that most of these donors support many charities per year.

- 94 per cent of Canadian direct mail donors had supported health charities that conducted research and/or provided services related to specific illnesses and diseases.

- 85 per cent gave to social services organizations.

- 80 per cent made contributions to hospitals or health care institutions.

- 72 per cent supported international development and aid organizations.

- 70 per cent made donations to religious-based organizations.

- 65 per cent supported environmental causes.

- 52 per cent had given to domestic disaster relief causes.

- 41 per cent gave to organizations advocating for human rights.

- 37 per cent supported arts and culture organizations.

- 36 per cent made gifts to educational institutions and causes.

- 32 per cent made political donations.

If Jacqueline is indeed typical, she probably has a very "diversified portfolio" of types of charities and causes she supports each year.

How does Jacqueline give?

As we said earlier, giving through the mail is Jacqueline's preferred giving method. But licking stamps and mailing cheques isn't the only way she gives. According to our poll:

- Despite all the negative talk about it, 60 per cent of Canadian direct mail donors also reported making charitable gifts in response to phone calls in the past year.

- 45 per cent had made contributions at their front doors in response to a door-to-door canvass on behalf of a charity. The survey didn't differentiate between volunteer and professionally-based canvass operations.

- Almost a quarter (24 per cent) had also given in response to "the media," which could include direct response television, paid ad campaigns, news stories or public service announcements.

- ◆ 15 per cent made contributions because they had been personally approached by a friend, neighbour or co-worker.

- ◆ Only one in 20 had responded to a charitable e-mail appeal. Our survey also found that a minority (39 per cent) of direct mail donors had Internet access and that only three per cent had ever made an online charitable contribution.

"Ordinary" donors?

Most of the survey results described Canadians who were pretty ordinary in their giving habits. We were somewhat surprised at the number of donors who supported many charities and at the percentage who made relatively large gifts. Other than that, there wasn't much that set these donors apart from their fellows at the base of the donor pyramid.

Or not?

There was one area of questioning that unearthed radical new potential for mega-giving from many of these ordinary donors. When we first read the poll results, we called and asked the polling company to double-check the figures. They were confirmed.

This is exciting stuff. Let's go there now.

CHAPTER SIX

The Iceberg Philanthropy frontier

The Eureka moment

Do you remember the story of Archimedes and the bathtub?

As legend has it, good old Archimedes tried to get into an over-filled tub one day and caused some of the water to overflow onto the floor. At that very moment, he shouted, "Eureka!"

Archimedes had just formulated the theory that an object will displace a volume of water equal to its own volume.

His Eureka moment reminds us of our Eureka moment when it came to legacy giving. Our poll of direct mail donors was designed for two specific purposes:

1. We wanted to build a detailed profile of the typical direct mail donor. And as you've read we found Jacqueline.

2. We were also curious to know whether typical direct mail donors were open to upgrading their giving. Specifically, we asked whether they'd be willing to consider moving up to monthly gifts, mid-level gifts (single gifts of $500 or more) or gifts in their wills.

When we asked about legacy giving (and by this we mean charitable bequests only) we were floored. Here's what we found:

- 97 per cent of direct mail donors are already aware that they can make legacy gifts to charity. All of those check boxes you've been putting on your direct mail reply coupons have done the awareness job big time.

- 91 per cent of the donors we surveyed already have a will. These numbers increase with the donors age, with 74 per cent of donors aged less than 55 having a will, 89 per cent of donors between age 55 and 64 have one, and a whopping 95 per cent of donors over the age of 65 have made a will.

- 48 per cent of direct mail donors said they thought that leaving legacy gifts to charity is a "good idea." Females (50 per cent of whom said it was a good idea) were more legacy-friendly than male donors (43 per cent).

- Here's the great news. Fully 17 per cent of the donors we surveyed had already named at least one charity in their wills! Unmarried donors and donors with no children not surprisingly scored well above the average score on this question, as did donors who give to 20 or more charities per year.

- We're not done with the great news just yet. Another 18 per cent of direct mail donors said that they were "very likely" or "somewhat likely" to name a charity in their wills in the future. A few segments scored significantly better than the norm on this question. They include:

- Females responded yes at twice the rate that males did.

- Donors who give to 20 or more charities per year are twice as likely to answer yes to this question as donors who give to five or fewer charities.

- Donors with a university education responded yes at twice the rate of those with high school or college education.

◈ Finally, a majority of direct mail donors (51 per cent) said that no charity has ever asked them to make a charitable gift in their wills.

Show me the money!

Let's take a minute and do some arithmetic. Let's figure out how much legacy revenue could be hiding within your donor pyramid. Put another way, let's estimate how much money is going unnoticed below your iceberg's waterline.

In the interest of transparency, we want to separate fact from supposition here. This requires making some assumptions in order to calculate revenue potential. You should feel free to adjust these assumptions to best fit your reality.

◈ 17 per cent of the donors surveyed said they'd left bequests to charities already. We're prepared to take them at their word. If you wish, you can discount this percentage to some degree. But in our judgment, this figure should be solid.

◆   Our research didn't tell us how many charitable bequests each individual donor had made. In other words, we counted donors and not gifts. We know anecdotally that donors often make multiple legacy gifts and, in some cases, they make many within one will. We think that two charitable bequests per donor is a reasonable estimate.

◆   Next we need to establish an average bequest value. Again no one to our knowledge has measured this scientifically. Having said that, we talk to lots and lots of planned giving fundraisers and our best estimate is that the average Canadian bequest to charity has a value of $20,000. Hospitals are the exception to this. Their bequests seem to be double this figure.

◆   Now to the most challenging piece of the equation. In our research, 18 per cent of donors surveyed said that they were either "very likely" or "somewhat likely" to make a charitable bequest in the future. Here's where a good dose of intuition needs to come into play. In our judgment, this number needs to be discounted – simply because we don't always follow through on our intentions. (What's your track record with New Year's resolutions?). We're comfortable assuming that one-third of this group will actually follow through with a legacy gift at some point in the future.

Let's walk it through with Save the Pussycats

Save the Pussycats Canada is the name we'll give to a real charity we talked to recently. SPC has been running a successful direct mail program for years now. It has an active direct mail donor base of 90,000 single gift donors. Let's run our numbers through with SPC and see what kind of legacy revenue they're sitting on.

* 17 per cent of active SPC donors have already left charitable bequests. That adds up to 15,300 donors who've made bequests.

* 18 per cent of SPC donors say they're likely to make charitable bequests in the future. We've decided to reduce this number to six per cent. So, a further 5,400 SPC donors will leave bequests to charity in the future.

* Adding the two together, we end up with 20,700 SPC donors who have made or will make charitable bequests.

* With an average bequest gift amount of $20,000, SPC donors will leave at least $414 million in their wills to the charities of their choice.

That's a lot of money — an awful lot.

So has Save the Pussycats seen this potential? Not really. When we last spoke to SPC's planned giving officer, she told us that she is currently cultivating and stewarding about 250 prospects and expectancies (which is typical from the planned giving officers we've talked to in the last few years). Simply put, SPC is missing the boat.

SPC doesn't yet begin to get what Iceberg Philanthropy is all about.

But let's get back to the math. If you want to get your head around your legacy revenue potential, simply multiply your number of active direct mail donors by $920. If you read this book and do adopt the strategies and tactics in it, you could well do better than that. If you let your competition get there first, you'll probably come up short.

Looking ahead

If nothing changed in the future, SPC would do just fine, thank you. You'll recall that the average Canadian direct mail donor supports 10 charities per year. SPC donors will give a total of $828 million in their wills. If SPC gets its 10 per cent of this money, they would receive just under $83 million without lifting a finger. That's pretty sweet.

But it won't play out that way.

Think of playing Monopoly. Everybody starts out equally – but things don't stay equal for very long.

Over the next 10 years some charities will see their Iceberg potential and go after legacy gifts with a vengeance. Other charities will stick with the status quo and do very little if anything to market legacy gifts below the waterline.

Those that get serious about Iceberg Philanthropy will expand their legacy donor constituencies – at the expense of those who do little or nothing. This is simply the way markets work. Remember when we talked about the cycle of innovation? The innovators, early adopters and laggards? Legacy giving in Canada will follow this natural law of markets.

We wrote this book so that you can see the potential Iceberg Philanthropy offers your organization and so that you can act now to maximize your legacy revenues down the road.

The legacy revenue view from 37,000 feet

Let's expand our scope now and do our best to estimate the legacy revenue potential from those direct mail donors who are giving in Canada today.

In recent years, we've been measuring the size of Canada's direct mail market. We've contracted with Decima Research – a brand name Canadian polling firm – to ask 2,000 Canadians over age 18 whether they give to charity in the mail. This research is considered accurate plus or minus 2.2 per cent, 19 times out of 20.

In 2006 this research found that 28 per cent of Canadian adults reported making charitable gifts in the mail in response to appeals they'd received in the mail. According to Statistics Canada, there were 26.62 million adults in Canada in 2006. By combining the two figures we can infer that 7.5 million Canadian adults made direct mail donations to charity in 2006.

We went on to ask this large sample of Canadian adults if they had left a bequest to charity and 10.2 per cent of direct mail donors reported having done so. It's worth noting that only 4.9 per cent of non-direct mail donors had made charitable bequests. Therefore, direct mail donors are twice as likely to make charitable bequests as people who don't give through the mail.

So let's do the arithmetic again – this time on a macro scale:

- ◈ 765,000 Canadian direct mail donors have made charitable bequests.

- ◈ Even if each donor only makes one bequest – with an average gift amount of $20,000 – we arrive at a total of $15.3 billion. That's $15,300,000,000. Talk about a lot of zeroes!

- ◈ This research didn't ask about people's intentions to make bequests in the future. If the pattern from our earlier research holds true, we'd end up with a figure in excess of $20 billion.

We've also done research on life expectancy and direct mail donors. Take a second and recall Jacqueline's profile. By and large, direct mail donors were alive during the Second World War. Without getting into excessive detail, this money will be realized (meaning the donors in question will die) within the next 15 years.

Thus, charitable giving in bequests will amount to about a billion dollars a year over the next 15 to 20 years. By the way, we estimate that Canadians give about a billion dollars a year through the mail. We're talking about a market that's just as big as direct mail. That's a big honkin' iceberg!

Here's some food for thought:

- ◈ How much time and money are you spending on your direct mail program this year?

- How much time and money are you willing to spend to double this revenue over the next 15 years?

- Direct mail programs typically spend a dollar to make two to three dollars over the course of a year. Legacy marketing pays off at a ratio of 20 to one or better. When it comes to efficiency, there's no comparison. On the other hand, the direct mail revenue comes in during the same fiscal year in which the investment is made. Iceberg Philanthropy requires a lot more patience. Most charities have such a need for instant gratification that they can't or won't make the long-term legacy investment. If you're smart and strategic, you'll make this work to your advantage by getting a jump on your competition.

- The typical $35-per-year direct mail donor would have to give for 571 years to match the donor who leaves a $20,000 gift in her will.

Pass the Tylenol. By now, your head is probably hurting from the scope of the numbers we've been throwing at you. Relax, your reaction is normal.

When we first started running these numbers ourselves, we kept going back to repeat our calculations. We simply couldn't believe that the revenue dollars could be that huge. Having said that, we trust our research. We've gone to great pains to conduct our research using nothing but best practices – and taking no shortcuts.

Our first reaction was to be overwhelmed at the possibilities. But, after the initial shock of the immense legacy potential from Canadian direct mail donors, we became very excited about bringing this potential to life.

CHAPTER SEVEN

Finding prospects

When we started our research into Iceberg Philanthropy we were surprised at how little has been written about legacy prospect identification. For example, while the "texts" used in the planned giving profession went into great detail about planned giving vehicles, very little has been written about who to talk to about this stuff in the first place.

Conference presenters typically talk about "working concentric circles." The planned giving officer first approaches current board members. Next she talks to former board members, then senior volunteers, then senior staff, and so on.

This approach makes very good sense as far as it goes. If your goal is to make the most of your face time on a one-on-one basis, this inside-out approach will probably yield the greatest number of expectancies and prospects per hour of time spent on the effort.

The problem with this approach is that it is very limited. And it doesn't even start to tap the potential we've been outlining to you in the previous chapter. You can also bet dollars to donuts that any planned giving officer using this approach is never going to make it to Jacqueline – and the thousands like her – who are literally ripe for a conversation about a gift in the will.

Put another way, the "concentric" approach keeps the focus well above the waterline and ignores the massive potential that lies below. Our earlier discussion about Save the Pussycats Canada illustrates this point perfectly. The planned giving officer is working a few hundred relationships when she should be engaged with tens of thousands of her donors. Failing to reach those *below the waterline* donors will cost Save the Pussycats millions of dollars of lost revenue in the years to come.

There's a fundamental problem in the conventional wisdom of the planned giving sector. And we want to address that problem as clearly — and bluntly — as we possibly can.

Problem: The assumption that planned giving is such a personal matter that suspects and prospects must be related to on a one-to-one basis. We call this the *tea and banana bread syndrome*. Planned giving professionals are taught (over and over again) that they must sit in the donor's living room and discuss planned giving in long, individualized conversations.

Solution: We introduced a pretty revolutionary concept in Chapter 2, namely that you can market legacy gifts to your donors. Mass communications techniques can be employed effectively and efficiently to reach the large numbers of donors who have the potential to make gifts to you in their wills. In fact, as we'll explain later, the majority of donors below your iceberg's waterline want it this way.

Please don't read on until you truly grasp this idea. You don't have to agree with it just yet. We'll convince you later. But please understand it fully.

We'll restate our case again briefly:

- 48 per cent of your ordinary direct mail donors think that leaving a gift to charity in their wills is a good idea.

- Traditional one-on-one conversations and relationships will allow you to engage with a couple of hundred donors – when you need to reach thousands.

- The key to success in Iceberg Philanthropy involves a paradigm shift, namely marketing legacy gifts to these donors instead of having tea and banana bread in their living rooms.

- As we'll show you soon, donors like Jacqueline prefer a marketing approach. They're used to a less personal relationship with you. In fact, they don't want you ringing their doorbells.

- Making this paradigm shift will enable your organization to get its share of the $15 billion that will be up for grabs in the decade to come.

Got it? Good.

The four-legged stool

So, if the "concentric circle" approach is the wrong way to find Iceberg Philanthropy prospects, what's the right way?

After years of research (and, yes, some trial and error), we've narrowed ourselves down to four key criteria. So here's our recipe for prospect identification below the waterline (where those billions are).

1. Start with age

When we were first starting out with the idea of Iceberg Philanthropy, we did some donor focus groups on behalf of an Ontario teaching hospital. A focus group is a two-hour, facilitator-led discussion around a board-room table. Each group typically includes eight to 12 participants.

We had contracted with this hospital to conduct two discussion groups and decided to conduct the first group with participants who were married and the second group with unmarried participants.

As it turned out, the married group all appeared to be between 45 and 60 years of age, while members of the unmarried group were over 65.

We asked both groups the question, "When you think of the word legacy, what do you think it means to your life?" The first two responders in the younger group said something like, "It means I'm going to die and I don't want to think about it." Members of the older group on the other hand all had thoughtful and articulate answers. In fact, one woman said, "My legacy is the footprint I'll leave on this world when I'm gone."

There was a clear difference between the groups. The older/unmarried group was prepared to talk about the end of their lives – while the younger/married group simply didn't want to go there.

Through further research and testing, we found that the differentiating factor between the groups wasn't marital status. Rather it was the age of the participants. We have become convinced that people accept their own mortality at a certain age. In our opinion, that age is somewhere around 65.

We found an article in *The Journal of Palliative Care** that gave us some very good clues. In essence, the article said that people accept their own impending death once they have experienced some deaths within their peer group.

So let's take it back to Jacqueline. She's lost a sister to breast cancer. Her best friend from high school is gone. Her next door neighbour who was the same age — they'd raised their kids together in the same neighbourhood for 25 years — passed away two years ago. Jacqueline has reached the point in her life's journey where she accepts that death is a part of life. In our view, Jacqueline is now ready to make charitable bequests in her will. She's ready to think about the footprint she'll leave on this earth – a footprint that reflects her life's values and priorities.

Let's recall Chapter 1 for a moment. Demographer David Foot says that demographics are two-thirds of everything. Communications expert Bernie Gauthier says that age separates us far more than geography.

After all our research and experimentation we're prepared to state this:

Legacy gift prospects within your iceberg are going to be found among those of the Civic generation. In other

---

* *Journal of Palliative Care*, "Providing Palliative Care to Older Adults: Context and Challenges", Margaret M. Ross, Associate Professor, University of Ottawa, Community Researcher, Victorian Order of Nurses Canada, and Beth McDonald, Executive Director, Victorian Order of Nurses, Ottawa-Carleton Branch; 10:04 Winter 1994; Pages 5-10.

words, your bequest prospects were born before or during the Second World War.

Conventional planned giving orthodoxy would disagree with us. Most traditional planned giving professionals would argue that we've focused in on donors who are older than need be and that people in their 40s and 50s make good planned giving prospects.

They might well be right if you're still focused at the tip of your iceberg – and only talking to board members and senior volunteers. These people may have the means, and the depth of attachment to your cause, to make such gifts. But we argue vehemently that those ordinary donors like Jacqueline who are below the waterline will probably consider a bequest to you once they're in their sixties – and not before.

2. *The hit parade*

The second factor in determining a donor's likelihood of becoming a bequest prospect is pretty simple. Does she love you?

As our polling found, the typical direct mail donor gives to some 10 charities per year. It stands to reason that each donor has favourites among those 10 – and that she'll leave her bequest(s) to those at the top of her *most favourite* list. This list is what we call the "hit parade."

Our rule of thumb is pretty simple. If your organization is one of your donor's top three charities of choice, you're in the ballgame to go after a gift in her will. If you're number nine or 10, your chances of a bequest are probably pretty remote. Having said that, if you're asking and no one else is, you'll no doubt beat the odds and get some.

To simplify to the greatest degree possible, making their "hit parade" really boils down to a couple of key issues:

⬧ The donor is deeply committed to your cause. This factor is external to your organization *per se* – but rather is totally related to the field of endeavour you work within. Jacqueline lost her mother and sister to breast cancer. She has deep feelings (remember subconscious giving from Chapter 4?) about the issue.

   Someone who did a two-year overseas volunteer stint with an international development NGO in the 1960s could be a prospect for an aid or development organization. Other donors might be deeply rooted to their community hospital or their alma mater.

⬧ The donor has great faith and trust in your organization and in the impact it has on the cause in question. She believes implicitly that you have vision, that you make a difference, that you manage her donations well and that you'll still be doing these things 10 or 20 years from now. We'll get into more detail on this later.

3. *Open to bequests*

This one's also very straightforward. The donor must be open to leaving legacy gifts in order to become a prospect. If she feels a gut resistance to charitable gifts in wills, you're probably best to just leave her alone.

There's an old maxim in marketing that goes, "It's much easier to create a perception than to change one." If a donor has developed an *anti-bequest attitude*, it will take a lot of money – and time – to change that perception. And you'll only change perceptions with a very small minority of those you go to work on.

The good news here is that almost half of ordinary direct mail donors like Jacqueline are in fact open to leaving charitable bequests.

4. *Family comes first usually*

The final leg of the stool involves what we call "family circumstance." This boils down to three simple components of the donor's family makeup, namely:

- having a spouse or not
- the number and age of children
- the number and age of grandchildren.

Simply put, a donor who is married and who has a number of children and grandchildren is less likely to make a charitable bequest than a widowed donor with two children in their forties and no grandchildren.

We've done dozens of legacy focus groups with donors from a wide spectrum of charities. And we've spoken to hundreds of donors about their attitudes toward making legacy gifts. When the topic is first raised by the discussion moderator, the participants start talking about family first. They'll say things like:

◆ "I don't think I'd do that while Harry (the husband) is still alive."

◆ "I need to make sure my children are alright."

◆ "I feel obligated to take care of my grandkids and their education."

Obviously, if there's no spouse – and a smaller number of children and grandchildren – there's a smaller bridge for the donor to cross to conceptualize making charitable bequests.

We want to be clear here. We're not saying that married donors with children and grandchildren won't make legacy gifts. We're simply saying that fewer of them will and that it will take more work and money on your part to get them to the point of serious gift consideration. We'll talk more about helping them cross the *family bridge* shortly.

Become a legacy detective

We've outlined the four characteristics that separate the wheat from the chaff when it comes to identifying legacy prospects within your donor constituency. The question leads to another: how does one go about actually finding them? Here are some hints that we think you'll find useful.

But, before we start, there's an important item for you to consider. Gathering donor information first requires that you have set up your donor database to handle the input we're discussing in this chapter. So first make sure your software is capable of receiving the types of data we're about to discuss.

Age

- Look for the shaky handwriting scribbled on the reply coupons of your direct mail campaigns – or in the notes that donors send back.

- First names are a great clue. Women named Eunice, Doris, Beryl and Myrtle were probably of the 1940s or earlier age group. So are men named Walter, Franklin, and Bert. In fact, if you google a bit, you can find the most popular first names given to children on a decade-by-decade basis.

- Simply observe donors whenever you can. If you're having events – or have any opportunity to see donors face-to-face – make a note of those who appear to be in their sixties or older.

- As well, you should listen closely to your donors' voices when you speak with them on the telephone. While some people will fool you, it's pretty easy to estimate a donor's age simply by listening to her voice.

- Simply ask them how old they are.

Loyalty

Of the four legs to the prospect identification stool, this one is already largely recorded in your database. A simple review of a donor's giving history to your organization will pretty much tell you whether or not you're near the top of her hit parade.

◆ Look for consistent giving over time. One of our favourite techniques is to look for two gifts or more per year for a certain number of consecutive years. As few as three works.

◆ Longer-term monthly donors are also good suspects. Monthly donors who have stayed active for three to five years are demonstrating a pretty high degree of loyalty to your cause. Keep in mind that a majority of direct mail donors never make monthly gifts.

Note: Some charities have monthly donors who were originally acquired by direct response television, door-to-door canvass or on-the-street direct inter-cept. We have only worked with monthly donors who were originally acquired by mail or telephone and we have no research or experience-based evidence that DRTV or face-to-face acquired monthly donors make good legacy prospects.

◆ Large single gifts are also an indicator of legacy gift potential. Depending on your cause and donor base, you may want to look for donors who have given single gifts of $250 or more. If you're a larger charity, you may want to raise the bar to $500 gifts.

◆ The best way we know of to find out if you're one of the donor's favourite charities is to ask them straight up.

Openness to legacy giving

This is an attitudinal question that you can't read in the database tea leaves. Simply put, you must ask donors if they think leaving charitable bequests is a good idea.

♦ You can include a question to this effect on the reply device of your direct mail campaigns.

♦ Many of our direct mail clients do an annual donor survey as part of a solicitation package. The donor is asked both to make a gift and to tell us more about themselves and their attitudes toward the charity. These surveys consistently boost gift response, by the way. You can simply include a few questions about having wills, awareness of gifts in wills and whether or not these gifts are a good idea.

Family circumstance

Again the information in your current database probably won't give you any indication of a donor's likelihood of having a spouse, children or grandchildren.

The exception to this rule is the title "Miss." Older women who never married still use this form of address on their cheques and their correspondence. And, we can tell you from experience, that "Miss" donors should definitely be included in your legacy marketing program.

Again you can ask family questions as part of broader donor survey projects you undertake.

Everyone in your shop should keep their antennae up for any family or marital information the donor may volunteer as part of her day-to-day conversations with you.

(Note: Please keep privacy ethics – and law – firmly in mind as you do your detective work. Our rule of thumb is only to keep data on a donor that you would be willing to have her look at. Remember we're trying to build relationships here – and not take advantage of them.)

The all-in-one solution

Our preferred method of gathering all this information is by doing prospect identification over the phone. Here's how it works:

- We start by selecting donors from the database who meet some of the criteria outlined above. We might pick "Miss" donors, donors who have made large single gifts, donors with a long-term, consistent giving history and monthly donors who have been active for a certain period of time.

- We then set up a phone campaign. We call the selected donors and ask if we might interview them for seven or eight minutes. We're clear that we're gathering individual information about them. We don't pretend that we're conducting an anonymous survey or poll.

- We then ask a series of multiple-choice questions of the donors who agree to participate. Each answer to these questions is assigned a numerical weight. At the end of the interview, each donor has achieved a "score" with respect to their likelihood of making a legacy gift.

It might surprise you, but this approach works very well indeed. Very few donors complain to the charity about perceived intrusions into their privacy.

Here's a sense of the metrics of this approach. Let's assume we start the prospect identification campaign with 5,000 donors who have been selected as outlined above.

◆ Assuming the data is in decent shape, we'll reach about 85 per cent of them by phone. Keep in mind that older donors are less likely to have caller I.D. and other tools provided by today's home telephone suppliers. So, of the original 5,000 names, we'll actually talk to about 4,250 of them.

◆ Of the 4,250 donors we reach, half will agree to answer the interview questions. That's 2,125 completed interviews – and a lot of valuable information for you to input into your donor database.

◆ Of the 2,125 donors who complete the interviews, a quarter will self-identify as legacy prospects. To oversimplify somewhat, the scores from their answers indicate that

• The charity in question is one of their favourites.

• They like the idea of leaving gifts to charities in their wills.

• Their family circumstances don't overly obstruct their ability to make legacy gifts.

In this example, we'll end up with 531 donors who have self-identified as being very good legacy gift prospects.

These are the people the charity should begin to cultivate – and eventually solicit – in a planned and organized way.

You can vary the number of donors you begin with, depending on the size of your donor database, the budget you have available and the urgency with which you embrace the Iceberg Philanthropy approach outlined in this book.

It certainly makes sense to do a test run first and see how it goes. If you're happy with the outcome, you can certainly roll out and expand your reach next year.

Fish hooks and big nets

Think of legacy fundraising as fishing. The traditional approach in the fundraising profession has been to fish with a line and a hook – and catch one fish at a time. Iceberg Philanthropy is all about fishing with a net. A big net. Done properly, there's no reason whatsoever that you shouldn't be identifying new bequests by the dozen.

It's a stretch. We know because we've had to stretch our own minds away from what we were originally taught. Iceberg Philanthropy flies in the face of just about everything we were taught in planned giving books, articles and seminars. But stretching is good for you. It might hurt a bit at first. Think of it as planned giving yoga. Embrace it and you'll be rewarded.

CHAPTER EIGHT

First principles

Now it's time to start putting the rubber onto the road.

Up to this point we've made our case for innovation in your planned giving and/or direct marketing program. We've shown you a huge new batch of "ordinary" donors with tremendous legacy potential. And we hope we've convinced you that they're worth the effort and your attention. After all, they're going to leave some $15.3 billion. And you want to earn some of that, right?

But, as we've been saying, if you want to successfully connect with Jacqueline – and 7.5 million donors like her – you have to use a strategic approach. Iceberg Philanthropy offers you that strategy.

You'll have lots of flexibility as to your tactical plan, depending on factors unique to your organization. Having said that, there are two – and only two — principles that you must adhere to religiously if you want to generate the full potential that Iceberg Philanthropy has to offer you. Let's take a look at these principles now.

1. It's all in the will

Take a look at a dozen planned giving brochures from a wide variety of charitable and/or non-profit organizations. Look specifically at the number of methods of planned giving they talk about. Charitable remainder trusts. Gifts of insurance. Gifts of appreciated securities. Annuities. We've looked at brochures that describe (some in mind-numbing detail) seven or more ways in which the donor can make a planned gift.

Now, e-mail a half dozen fundraising colleagues who are involved in planned giving in some way. Ask them where their planned giving money actually comes from.

We've been asking fundraisers this question for years. And, without exception, they answer in one of the following three ways:

- 90 per cent or more of our planned giving revenue comes from bequests.

- 95 per cent or more of our planned giving revenue comes from bequests.

- All our planned giving revenue comes from bequests.

So we have a very simple question for you to ponder: *If 90 per cent or more of the planned giving revenue out there comes from bequests, why do you even talk about the other stuff?*

Direct marketers understand the rule of singularity. They know that the most effective offers combine one specific need and one specific ask. They know how to keep it specific – and to keep it simple. They know that the donor understands the offer best when it's singular.

For some reason, and we're not sure why, the planned giving branch of fundraising is different. These folks seem compelled to offer the donor a virtual dim sum menu of quite complicated choices and options.

Iceberg Philanthropy is all about making it easy for Jacqueline to leave your organization a lot of money. After years of listening to hundreds of ordinary donors just like her, we are convinced simplicity and singularity work best.

Some of you are no doubt wrestling with this idea in your heads right now. Let's construct a scenario, using Save the Pussycats Canada as our charity in question.

SPC is planning to include a planned giving insert in all of its tax receipt mailings to donors next year. Staff member Jane was at a conference three months ago and learned all about planned giving vehicles. She wants the insert to describe these vehicles to the donor. Staff member Ingrid has just finished reading this book. She's convinced that the insert should stay focused exclusively on wills and bequests.

Jane wins the debate. The insert talks about six vehicles and their tax advantages. One donor indicates an interest in a gift of insurance. However, the majority of the SPC donors getting receipts glance at the insert and put it down without reading it. To them, the thought of reading the insert seems too much like work. Jane might get one insurance gift. But she loses the "mind share" of thousands of donors.

Opportunity lost.

Now, let's imagine that Ingrid wins the debate. The insert talks about the mission of the organization and invites donors to make a bequest. Full stop. Granted SPC might lose an insurance gift. But in this case, almost all of the donors getting receipts actually read the insert. In the following weeks, SPC gets three bequest confirmations and 38 requests for more information on leaving gifts in wills.

Opportunity seized.

In marketing, this is called the Law of Sacrifice. Simply put, this law works like this: *In order to really get what you want, you've got to give something up.*

Light beers give up one per cent of alcohol to dramatically reduce the number of calories per bottle. Smart cars give up interior room to get better gas mileage.

Light beer makers aren't really after fewer calories. They're after the beer drinkers who are concerned about their waistlines. Smart carmakers aren't really after lower mileage. They're after the drivers who care about green-house gas emissions (and perhaps the cost of fuel).

Get the idea?

At the end of the day, the sacrifice we're asking for is a very small one. After all, we're asking you to give up a tiny percentage of potential revenue in order to gain a much bigger share of the "90 per cent-plus pie."

No-brainer, isn't it? So please, keep it simple. Jacqueline likes it that way!

2. *Poets or tax accountants?*

Now go back to that pile of planned giving brochures you've collected. Take a minute to look them over and ask yourself, "Were these written by a poet or a tax accountant?"

We'll be very surprised if your response is "poet" to *any* of the brochures.

Now we're not fundraising historians, but we've constructed our own scenario about the earliest days of the practice of planned giving.

Once upon a time, there was a charity called Save the Pussycats Canada. Thirty-two years ago, SPC received three charitable bequests from its donors in a period of just three weeks.

The chair of the Fundraising Committee at SPC had a great idea. "If gifts like these come to us without any effort on our part, what might happen if we actually promote this kind of giving?"

She went home and told her husband (who was an accountant) about her new idea. He was also enthused – and offered some helpful advice. "Honey, do you remember Fred from last year's company golf tournament? He knows something about estate planning. Why don't you invite him to your next committee meeting, and he can tell you how this stuff works?"

She took his advice. Fred came to the meeting and gave the committee a briefing on the ins and outs of how donors can leave "planned gifts" to charity.

The planned giving industry was born.

For the past 30 years, we've been heeding Fred's advice. And, the truth be told, we in the charitable sector have had considerable success using Fred's approach. But – and it's a big but – there's a huge problem with all this. *Fred had never heard of Jacqueline!*

If the fundraiser from SPC had been married to a communications specialist or a marketer, this story could have turned out very differently indeed.

You see, Fred's clientele came from the upper economic strata of society. They were worth millions. They were looking for maximum tax avoidance – and were very savvy financial investors. They managed their portfolios actively and were very motivated to have their names appear on the new donor wall at the community hospital.

Let's go back to our iceberg. The donors Fred was thinking of were at its very peak. They were well above the waterline. They represented about one per cent of all the donors that gave to SPC that year.

Zoom ahead to the present day and the information you've already inputted into your brain from the reading you've done so far.

Bequests don't just come from the wealthy. In fact, $15.3 billion worth of these gifts are going to come from the very ordinary donors like Jacqueline who are flying well below everyone's radar. Those $30 donors have $20,000 potential. And most of them haven't even been asked for a legacy gift!

If that fundraiser in the story had come to us for advice, we would have pointed her in a very different direction. Our advice would look something like this:

- Find out as much as you can about your donors. Who they are. How they give. Why they support you.

- Get very clear about why they started giving to you in the first place – and keep your focus right there. Amplify and simplify that motivation.

◈ Talk to your donors about why they should leave a bequest and not how they can do it. Your donors are hungry for motivation – and not an instruction manual.

◈ Radiate passion for the cause. Remember that we're all emotional beings – and that we make our decisions with the amygdala, not the cerebral cortex.

◈ Remember that you're working on building relationships – and not running a tax planning seminar.

When we conduct legacy giving workshops, we often ask participants to role-play in an exercise we call "The Marriage Proposal." It goes like this.

We ask for four volunteers from the group. When we have our four, we select two "proposers" and two "proposees." Then we add a twist.

We ask one of the people making a marriage proposal to do it romantically – as if he were a poet. Then we ask the other proposer to construct a marriage proposal "like a tax accountant." This proposer is asked to focus on finances, tax breaks and numbers.

The results are hilarious. Within 10 minutes the entire room is cracking up with laughter. Here's what these proposals often sound like.

The poet

Rachel, when I look into your eyes I see the sky, the sea and the universe. You have given me a love the likes of which I've never known. My life, my heart,

*my soul have reached out and joined with yours. My
greatest joy is waking up to see you beside me – the
rhythm of your breath pulsing life into my day.*

*I want to share the rest of my existence on this
earth with you. I want to give you this incredible love
in my soul for the rest of my life.*

*Please marry me. Say yes, and make this the
happiest moment in my life.*

The tax accountant

*Rachel, I stayed up late last night working on
a spreadsheet. I looked at our respective financial
situations individually – and then I examined the
potential of a fiscal merger.*

*Rachel, our getting married simply makes a great
deal of sense from just about every angle.*

*By making one mortgage payment instead of two,
we can both pay off the house 10 years earlier and
maximize our RRSP contributions. We can also save
up to $2,500 per year on utilities.*

*I've also looked into the child tax credit and it
looks like we can have two children without compro-
mising our standard of living.*

*So what do you say? Would you like to marry
me?*

People are people. We don't change just because we
"put on our donor hat." We're emotional beings. Loving
and being loved is what gives true meaning to our lives.
Iceberg Philanthropy realizes that simple truth. So should
you.

So change your planned giving approach to focus on two very simple principles:

- ◆ Stay focused on the will – and the will only.

- ◆ Communicate with passion.

Do these two things well, and you're on your way. Stay focused on these principles and you'll connect with Jacqueline's heart and soul. And the money will follow.

CHAPTER NINE
Major gift strategy: direct marketing tactics

Remember our earlier discussion in Chapter 2 of the various levels at which fundraising works? When it comes to the people who give, we had tippers, buyers, donors and investors. On the fundraising side, we had selling, marketing and relating.

The orthodoxy of the "fundraising church" is that we sell to tippers and buyers, market to donors and relate with investors.

This book is about a new way to connect. It's about marketing investment giving and transforming very ordinary donors into substantial investors.

Courtship strategy

The strategy behind Iceberg Philanthropy has its roots deeply imbedded in the best practices employed by capital campaigners, major gift fundraisers and gift planners.

We think that the major gift process is much like a romantic courtship. Start out slow. Listen and watch for signs of reciprocation. Always be respectful. Never, ever hurry. Keep your eye on the prize. And invest what it takes to win.

◆ Suspects are identified from a larger pool of donors according to the linkage, ability and interest (LAI) criteria everyone studies when they prepare for their CFRE exams.

◆ A qualification process narrows the pool of suspects to a smaller group of prospects who have the greatest propensity to give at the level we're campaigning for – in this case, gifts in wills.

◆ Qualified prospects are strategically, carefully and patiently cultivated along the path to the legacy gift decision or sometimes the decision to tell you about the gift!

◆ When the time and circumstance appear optimal, an appropriate and respectful ask is made. The ask combines firmness and clarity on the part of the solicitor, along with a high degree of sensitivity to the prospect in question.

◆ Once a response to the solicitation is given, ensure that the donor receives further moves that will continue to grow the relationship. Depending on that answer, those moves could be stewarding the new gift, continuing cultivation in the hope of a gift in the future or accepting no and returning that donor to her previous relationship with your organization.

Wholesale tactics

While the strategy we've just described is clearly *major gift* in its nature, the tactics Iceberg Philanthropy employs are decidedly from the direct marketing world:

- Communications with the prospects are grouped, rather than individualized. Although, as with any good direct marketing, they should appear to speak to the individual.

- More emphasis is placed on the efficiencies created by communicating with groups of donors at once – rather than the tea and banana bread approach we described earlier.

- The process is data-reliant. It does not provide the fundraiser the ability to remember every exchange, every move and every prospect.

- There's no eyeball-to-eyeball opportunity for the fundraiser to read nuances, like facial expression and body language.

Bringing two camps together

In our experience, the Iceberg Philanthropy approach requires mental flexibility on the part of just about every fundraiser.

The fundraiser who comes from a major gift or planned giving background often struggles with distance. She feels discomfort with the idea that she doesn't get to talk to and listen to the prospect. She wants to employ her interpersonal skills to maximum advantage in the cultivation and solicitation process. The idea of dealing with hundreds — or thousands — of donors at a time can positively make her squirm.

By the same token, the fundraiser from the direct marketing world goes through his own contortions. He's used to instant gratification. He's in the asking – not cultivation – business. This all feels soft and mushy to him.

Fundraisers from both camps need to change their outlooks to make Iceberg Philanthropy work:

◆ Major gift and planned giving types need to fully grasp the simple idea that in order to communicate with all those ordinary donors below the water-line they have to communicate in much greater quantity – and less personally. They need to leap across the canyon from a "retail" to a "wholesale" approach.

◆ Direct marketers need to understand that the gift in question is light years bigger than anything they've ever asked for in the past. They need to redefine their interpretation of the word "campaign" to include multiple mailings. And they need to accept that they just can't be shouting a solicitation on every page of every letter.

We understand that Iceberg Philanthropy represents a change in the way you do your work, no matter what type of fundraising you've done in the past. Change rarely comes easily and it probably won't be easy for you.

Our best encouragement for you to change is to remind you of what's available if you make the change.

Direct mail donors will leave at least $15.3 billion worth of bequests to charity in Canada over the next 15 years.

You either want some of it or you don't. If you want your share, you're going to have to give up some old thinking and embrace some new and innovative approaches. Welcome to today, where the only constant appears to be change.

So start talking the talk. And let's move ahead to walking the walk.

Iceberg architecture

Any building project starts with a blueprint. Any solid fundraising campaign starts with a plan.

Your plan and its complexity will vary depending on many factors, including:

- How many donors your organization has.

- Your budget constraints over the next two or three years.

- The time you have available to commit to Iceberg Philanthropy.

- Your organization's cultural tolerance for risk and innovation.

- The state of your database and your ability to use it well.

- The ability of your direct marketing and planned giving functions to communicate and cooperate with each other.

This list could be much longer. We simply want to point out that this isn't a recipe for pot roast. Every organization, every fundraiser and every donor constituency is unique in some way. Your uniqueness should inform the way in which you draw the blueprint that's going to offer you the greatest opportunity for success.

Having said that, we have learned that there are four *foundational pillars* upon which Iceberg Philanthropy is built. These pillars run sequentially at first. When you get into the Iceberg groove over time, they'll all be happening simultaneously. Let's review those pillars now.

Research

This pillar or phase involves estimating, listening, identifying and qualifying. This is the period during which you'll gather invaluable information and narrow your margin of error for the phases to come.

The research function has several components:

◈ Selecting appropriate suspects from your donor constituency. We've given you the criteria already: age, loyalty, openness to bequests and family circumstance.

As we've already discussed, some of this information is readily available to you and some of it isn't. We believe that you can go to your donor base and select a great batch of legacy potentials based on your having read this book. Will your selections be perfect? Of course not. Why would they be?

In general somewhere around a third of your active direct mail donors are legacy potentials. We trust you to find your own way to whittle your database down to one in three. It's new, granted. But it's not rocket science.

◈ Active listening. There's an old saying that "we're all born with two ears, but only one mouth." Any TV psychologist would no doubt tell us that many relationships fail because one or both partners don't feel they were heard by the other. Before you start telling your donors about legacy gifts, it's critical that you listen to what they have to say on the subject. This can be done in a number of ways – both formal and informal.

Our preferred method for this listening is the use of qualitative research or focus groups. A small number of donors (eight to 12 works best, we think), who represent the criteria you've already selected, gather in a boardroom setting for a two-hour discussion facilitated by a moderator. We won't get into a full-blown discussion of how to run focus groups (that information is available elsewhere), other than to say that we've found them to be a highly effective tool in "taking the pulse" of donors and helping us refine and tailor legacy campaigns to really fit the charity in question.

◈ Prospect qualification. In order to make your campaign as efficient as possible, you'll want to narrow your initial pool to a smaller group of qualified prospects. Our rule of thumb is that your prospect list should be about one-quarter the size of your initial list of suspects.

As we've said earlier, the only way we know to do this is to ask them if they're prospects. Obviously, you don't just pop the question straight out, but you can ask a series of questions related to the four-legged stool we discussed in the previous chapter.

Our preferred methodology is to do this by means of telephone interviews of about seven minutes duration.

After talking with thousands of donors, we're continually surprised at how willing they are to share their attitudes, opinions, perceptions, wants and needs with you. It may sound trite but they're literally waiting for you to ask them!

Cultivation

Essentially this stage of the process involves introducing donors to the idea of making a legacy gift, making the case for a charitable bequest and inviting any feedback the donor wishes to give you.

Some guidelines you might find helpful include:

◆ Allowing about a year for this idea to gel with the donor. Patience is a virtue here. Space out your communications and allow the donor time to think and consult as she deems appropriate.

◆ Cultivate by mail. Hundreds of donors have told us in focus groups that they're willing to be approached about bequests. But they want to be approached by mail. Simply put, they feel intimidated by the idea of personal visits or phone calls. They'd rather sit at the breakfast table and read what you've got to say. They feel that this gives them the greatest degree of control over the relationship. And they don't want to give that control over to you.

* Stay focused on mission, program and future needs. We'll talk about this more shortly. For now, just remember to keep talking to them about the reasons why they give to you in the first place. In our experience, the donor will decide to leave a bequest for essentially the same reasons that she chose to send you that first $30 cheque in the mail.

* Don't overdo it. When you're designing and writing your cultivation packages, please avoid the temptation to get too glossy or too technical. Simple, honest and straightforward communication is what they want – and that's precisely what you should give them. Remember, you're talking to Jacqueline and not the CEO of some Fortune 500 corporation!

The ask

When we first designed the Iceberg approach, we called this part of the program "solicitation." With experience, we rethought this idea and we now prefer the word "identification."

Essentially when it comes to "popping the question," we believe it's more appropriate to ask the donor where she is in her decision-making process than to ask her for a gift *per se*.

The objective of the ask is to split your prospects into four new segments:

- Those who have already made a bequest and are prepared to tell you.

- Those who are actively considering a bequest to you but haven't yet added you to their will.

- Those who aren't really thinking about leaving a bequest to you at this point, but are open to receiving more bequest information in the future.

- Those who simply aren't interested and don't really want to hear more on the subject from you.

Taking stock

Once you've gone through these four stages the first time, it's time to pause, reflect, analyze and plan.

- At the most basic level, you'll need to lay out some kind of stewardship/communication plan for the group that has indicated that a bequest is already there for you.

- You'll want to keep cultivating the group that's considering a bequest and have a plan and date to re-approach them with the identification process.

- The third group, those for whom a bequest isn't on the front burner, also needs to continue to receive legacy gift information from you – so that when they're ready, you'll be top-of-mind.

- The "not interested" group can simply be put back into your regular annual direct mail program. You may want to flag these people so that you don't inadvertently pull their names again two years from now.

From campaign to process

This is also the point at which you should probably adjust your approach from a singular test campaign to making Iceberg Philanthropy an ongoing component of your annual fundraising program — and budget!

Not to make the donor seem like an industrial product, but think of a conveyor belt:

◆ Expectancies (people who've told you the gift is there) come off the belt and go onto a new steward-ship belt.

◆ The prospects who are interested but have not made a bequest get picked up at the end of the belt and moved back on the same belt to be cultivated some more and asked again, maybe in a year or two.

◆ The "back burner" prospects receive much the same treatment, except their cultivation moves may be less frequent and less expensive. Their next ask will be further in the future, maybe in three or four years.

The size, scope and cost of the conveyor belt process will vary with your organization, your donors, your budget and your perceptions of the success of your initial Iceberg campaign. Having said that, it's important at this point not just to turn the conveyor belt off and say, "We're done." You've raised the level of the relationship with some very important donors. You're getting the hang of how to do this. You've learned some valuable lessons about your donors.

How you do continue isn't as important as deciding that you will continue in the way that makes the most sense to you.

You'll also want to look at the original donor segments you started out with (i.e. loyal, monthly). Which group or two responded best? Now's the time to go back into your database and start the cultivation/identification process with more donors from those groups. Combine them with the "interested but no gift" group and the "back burner" group from your first campaign and repeat the process.

It's simple really.

Eye on the prize

There are only two things that really matter here:

◆ Start out doing the four pillars in sequence. Do your segment selection and research. Take a year or so to cultivate through the mail. Identify and segment responses as we've shown you. Then pause, analyze, plan and turn the conveyor belt back on. You can take all the liberties you like within these parameters. You can speed it up a bit or slow it down. You can start with two donor segments or six. You can do your first campaign with 50 donors or 25,000. Those are the tactical decisions that you can make better than we can.

◆ Once you've done your identification exercise the first time through, keep going! In our experience, this is one of the biggest pitfalls our clients fall into. They start mining their iceberg – maybe five per cent of it. They get very good results from the process. Everyone's happy. Then they stop and shift their attention to the spring golf tournament. Please remember two numbers: $15.3 billion and 15 years. If you practice Iceberg Philanthropy for a year and stop, you'll lose a lot of money. It's like fitness and dieting. Do it for 12 weeks and you'll look and feel better. Stop then and where will you be a year later? The same place you started.

We want to close this chapter by returning to the idea of behavioural change. It's almost never easy – for individuals or organizations.

Iceberg Philanthropy will require change on your part if you want it to work for you. If you summon the where-withal to put it into practice, you'll be remembered as a pioneer. And, in the years to come, your organization and your cause will have advanced to a new level because of the revenue generated by your vision.

CHAPTER TEN

Talking Jacqueline's talk

There's a great Far Side cartoon created by Gary Larson several years ago. The cartoon consists of two panels. Each panel has an identical drawing of a man scowling and pointing vigorously at his dog.

The first panel is titled "What man says" and the caption goes something like, "How many times have I told you, Prince! DO NOT bark at strangers! Bad dog! Bad dog!"

The second panel is titled "What dogs hear" and the caption reads "BLAH, BLAH, BLAH, BLAH."

The point of the cartoon, at least to us, is that even the most important messages you can deliver won't be heard if they're not easily understood.

The same principle applies to your donors. It especially applies to Jacqueline and the 7.5 million Canadian direct mail donors like her.

This chapter is all about how to talk to Jacqueline about leaving a legacy gift. We thought we'd present it to you as a laundry list of dos and don'ts – all related to the goal of connecting with Jacqueline in a meaningful and effective way.

These tips apply to all your legacy communications with ordinary direct mail donors. It doesn't matter if it's brochure copy, website content, the content of a cultivation letter or how you chat with her at a donor event.

The communications vehicle isn't as important as the audience. By and large, your direct mail donors are not worldly, wealthy, socially sophisticated members of the community's elite. Rather they are retired insurance company secretaries with grown kids who go to church. They don't see themselves as philanthropists – rather as ordinary people just trying to do a little good in the world.

At the risk of sounding immodest, we know these people better than anyone. We've been corresponding with them for years and years. We've conducted dozens of focus group discussions with hundreds of donors like Jacqueline. And we've talked about legacy gifts with well over 10,000 of them on the phone.

We've honed our skill at asking penetrating questions that get to the heart of the matter when it comes to legacy gifts. We've listened very hard to everything they've had to say in their responses. We've continually been impressed at their articulate answers, the depth of their commitment to humanity and their willingness to simply tell us what we want to know. When asked the right way, donors don't hold back when it comes to sharing their opinions, frustrations and aspirations.

So listen up! Jacqueline's about to tell you how to court her and maximize your chance of securing a gift for your organization in her will.

1. Never talk to these donors about "planned giving". This label means nothing to them. It doesn't make sense. Jacqueline has to work to understand it and has to ask for a definition. You don't want to make

Jacqueline work. You want to make it easy for her to consider a legacy gift to you.

Jacqueline is fine with other terms like "gift in will", "bequest" or "legacy gift".

Should the Canadian Association of Gift Planners change its name based on this? Nope. We as fundraisers can call it planned giving when we talk to each other. We just mustn't use this language when we talk to our donors!

2. Focus on why – not how. We've said before that Jacqueline needs inspiration to give more than she needs a "how to" instruction manual. You must make your case for a legacy gift. You must tell Jacqueline explicitly why her gift matters now and why it will matter in the future. She won't decide to give unless you jump through these hoops.

3. Show a credible vision of your organization in the future. Before leaving you a legacy, Jacqueline needs to believe that your organization will be around – and will still be filling an important need – well into the future.

You must articulate this future vision and be as explicit as you can about it. For example, the Chief of Medical Staff at a teaching hospital could articulate what cancer treatment might look like in 15 years as a result of the gene therapy research that's ongoing now. Or an educational psychologist could describe how new software programs currently being developed could allow dyslexics to read without difficulty.

4. Take vision to needs. Start with the vision of the future outlined above. But then make it more specific by describing the funding needs your organization will have 15 years from now. The organizations we've worked with have especially struggled with this one, so let's create an example.

HIV and AIDS have decimated a generation of adults in sub-Saharan Africa. Today orphaned children are either being raised by grannies or are raising their own siblings. Schools are recruiting twice as many teaching students as they'll eventually need as teachers because they assume that half the student teachers will die before they get a class of their own.

Today we have children without parents. Feeding, housing and educating these orphaned children is a massive challenge to humanity. But what will their needs be in the year 2020? How will they find work and achieve self-sufficiency if they're not sufficiently educated? How will they raise their own children when they didn't have parents of their own? Will many of them turn to prostitution and crime? What kinds of programs and initiatives will begin to solve these problems?

Perhaps community-based vocational training would help with the employment issue. Perhaps parenting education programs – combined with a mentoring program – could assist young adults to learn to be loving and effective parents.

Obviously we're not experts on HIV and AIDS or community-based capacity building. But the CEO of this NGO is. She needs to think about these issues and articulate specific pictures of what her organization's role might be in 10 or 20 years.

Another challenge is that when we approach the CEO in question for this kind of vision, she feels that we're asking for crystal balls and predictions. We don't expect predictions – nor does Jacqueline. Rather donors want to hear about plausible future scenarios and how their favourite charity will be relevant in engaging those scenarios to improve the human condition.

5. Talk about origins. Tell or remind your donors how your organization came into existence in the first place. What was the unmet need? Who had the idea? What was the initial vision? How did the first few pioneers build the organization? Talking about origins should take you directly to vision and mission – and Jacqueline likes that.

6. Big font. Older eyes start to fail. Keep the font readable for someone Jacqueline's age. We like 13 point as a rule. Do not give into the temptation to shrink the font in order to squeeze more words onto the page.

7. Hone your oratorical skills. Older donors respond really well to inspirational oratory. Boomers can be more skeptical. We once used Martin Luther King's "I have a dream" speech as a model upon which to write a vision piece for a hospital CEO. Older donors

ate it up. And yes, you can write brochure copy that sounds like a speech. Many donors listen to copy in their heads as they read.

8.   If you can, show previous legacy gifts at work. Tell the story of a bequest you've already received and how your organization used that gift to have measurable impact on furthering your cause.

In 1638 a man named John Harvard left a bequest of £780 and 400 books in his will. The instructions in his will were to use the books and the cash to establish an institution of higher learning in America. That modest legacy gift created what is now the strongest educational brand in the Western Hemisphere – Harvard University.

You probably don't have a bequest on file that matches that one for its impact. But that's not important. Perhaps a previous bequest built a new hospital wing, or established a scholarship program, or created a schoolyard garden program in Africa. It's worth the time to go back and find these stories if you have them.

And, if you have them, tell them to Jacqueline. She'll love them!

9.   Forego the gloss. Jacqueline wants good information on your organization and a good case as to why she should consider a gift in her will. She doesn't want you to go overboard with the production values of the material you send her. In fact, you'll annoy her if she thinks you've spent valuable dollars (or even cents)

trying to impress her. We've seen donors in focus groups whip each other into a near frenzy because they thought the materials they were reviewing were "too glossy and fancy." When we hear a donor ask, "How much did this cost?" in a focus group, we know we're headed for choppy water.

10. Use the right photos. Donors love pictures in printed legacy materials. But they don't love all pictures. Here are a couple of rules of thumb to keep in mind. First, use photos that show donor dollars at work. If you're a hospital, show a doctor at the bedside – not just standing and grinning at the camera. By the same token, if you're an international development NGO, show children with books walking to school – not a head and shoulders shot of those same children just smiling at the lens. If you're including a picture of someone who's giving a testimonial, keep it informal. Portrait-type shots don't work as well as more relaxed photos that look more like good snapshots.

11. Treat the donor as an individual. Yes, you're using mass marketing techniques to communicate Iceberg Philanthropy. But today's direct mail donor feels taken for granted. She feels like you're treating her as "one of the donor herd." And she resents it.

Think of the types of donors we've recommended to you as legacy gift prospects. They're either giving large gifts or they've been giving loyally for years. They feel they've earned a place as a legitimate stakeholder in your organization. And we think they're right to feel this way.

You need not go overboard with this. But adding some variable copy to a letter like, "You've been a loyal donor since 1990," or "You've made 25 gifts to Save the Pussycats in the past eight years," show the donor that you're aware of her individual role in advancing your cause.

Please don't be confused on this point. We're not saying the donor is seeking publicity or recognition. Jacqueline doesn't necessarily want to be on your donors' wall or have her name listed in your annual report. She's a modest one, that Jacqueline. She simply wants to be reassured that you know she exists and she's told us it's important for her to have that reassurance as she begins transitioning from active giving to thinking about a legacy gift.

12. Visual contrast. Older eyes have an easier time reading material when there are a lot of difference between type and background. Dark print on a white background is much easier on older eyes than reversed white type on a screened photo background.

This may seem a small issue. But it can be a real problem when a group of creative 30- and 40-somethings are reviewing draft materials. The design types want to show off their talents. The creative types want to get jiggy with it. The communications types want to invent impressive slogans.

The outcome of all this can be a disaster. What appeals to Gen-Xers often doesn't cut it with the Civic generation. People of Jacqueline's age don't need a lot of visual stimulation to stay engaged. Jacqueline didn't play Nintendo as a child.

Our advice? That group of staff members who want to be "creative" should invite their mothers or grand-mothers to the brainstorming session. We can pretty much guarantee that the outcome will be much more successful.

13. Give Jacqueline control of the relationship and be explicit about it. Tell her that you're sending her material because she's a loyal and valued donor. Tell her you think she may be interested in considering a legacy gift. Invite her to ask for more information. At the same time, invite her to tell you that she's not interested and you should stop sending her legacy materials. This approach shows respect and donors like Jacqueline are hungry for respect from the chari-ties they support.

14. Wear your heart on your sleeve. Don't be afraid to let your emotions show when you're writing any type of legacy giving communications. Let your writing show your love for your cause and your organization. This will trigger Jacqueline's love for you.

Remember that we humans are emotional animals. Remember the role of the amygdala in our decision-making process. Emotion drives impulse. Impulse drives decision. It's the emotional impulse that sets the whole thing in motion. Poets and tax accoun-tants, remember?

15. Have your written communications come from someone. Direct marketers understand that people respond to people. That's why every direct mail piece that lands in your mailbox is signed by an individual person. Yet, we'll bet that your planned giving brochures, if you have some, aren't from anyone. That's a mistake.

Most, if not all, of the messages in your materials should be from someone. The institutional messages can be from the CEO or the Chair of the Board of Directors. The personal messages can be from program recipients, like grateful hospital patients, or service deliverers, like the volunteer working on the HIV/AIDS project in Zambia.

16. Don't you dare tell Jacqueline that she needs to make a will. Direct mail donors have wills. Well okay, 92 per cent of them do. They're insulted by this kind of advice.

Having said that, it's quite all right to remind donors that it's a good idea to update wills regularly or when major life events take place.

17. Don't use someone else's brochure as your template. Almost all of the planned giving brochures out there today have it all wrong – at least when it comes to engaging the 7.5 million Canadian direct mail donors like Jacqueline.

18. Don't give them financial advice or dare to tell them how they should manage their own financial affairs. Charities do this all the time. And boy, does it ever

make donors angry! You can, if you wish, suggest that the donor consult her trusted advisors before making a legacy gift but that's as far as you can go.

19. When laying out your legacy print materials, take advantage of what Tom Ahern calls "the bouncing eye." Based on research by German professor Siegried Vöegle, Ahern tell us:

"Encountering an open newsletter or magazine, he discovered, the eye typically enters at the upper right-hand corner and moves immediately (and involuntarily) to the largest graphic on the page. The eye concludes its scan by exiting at the lower right-hand corner.

"That's the big picture. Vöegle also found that eyes go to:

⬥ *Photographs or drawings first, before they go to text.*

⬥ *Close-ups first, before they go to pictures showing the entire person.*

⬥ *Children first, before they go to adults.*

⬥ *Big text (i.e., headlines) first, before they go to small text.*

⬥ *Short words, short lines and short paragraphs first (i.e., headlines, captions, pull quotes)."**

---

* *Raising More Money With Newsletters Than You Ever Thought Possible*, by Tom Ahern, Emerson & Church Publishers, 2005.

20. Do show Jacqueline how you manage her money. Rather than talking to donors about how they should manage their affairs, show them that you do a superlative job of managing their donated dollars. Donors must have a high level of confidence in your organization's ability to get the best possible results with their dollar. If they don't have this confidence, they'll simply go elsewhere.

21. Tell stories. Tell lots of them. Use stories whenever and wherever you can to get your message across. We humans have been storytellers since time immemorial. We've been telling these stories because others of our species have loved listening to them.

    "The secret of success is to realize that at its heart fundraising is little more than telling great stories very well. And it is nothing less than the inspiration business. For we don't just ask for money, we inspire it. In no arena of fundraising is this truer than in the raising of bequests." — British fundraiser and relationship fundraising guru Ken Burnett

    Organizations like AFP and CAGP are starting to include conference sessions on narrative and storytelling. We applaud this. Telling – and listening to – stories is a primitive, basic and essential component of any relationship. It's fundamental to being human.

    Your life is full of stories. Think of the books you read recreationally, be they fiction or non-fiction. Every movie tells a story. Television is a story medium, whether it's the nightly news, night-time dramas or soap operas. People in Cape Breton Island who watch soaps say, "I'm watching the stories." There are stories on websites, in blogs and in chat rooms. You and your kids tell stories at the dinner table. Effective teachers use stories to educate children.

You can tell the story of your organization's beginnings. You can tell the story of an important program or service you offer or plan to offer in the future. Great donor profiles and donor testimonials take story form. If you work at a university, every student, every alumnus, every professor and every parent has a story to tell. Find these stories and tell them with flair. Jacqueline will eat them up.

So there you have it. These are our top 21 tips to get your legacy messages across to Jacqueline in a way that she'll appreciate and hopefully respond to.

If you think about it, every single tip in this list makes sense. Just think of your mom, your grandmother or an elderly aunt. Get inside her skin and look at the world the way she sees it.

Talking with her in the way we've just described will get you well on your way to your share of the $15.3 billion that's up for grabs right now.

We would like to acknowledge British legacy fundraising legend Richard Radcliffe for his contributions to tips 8, 10, 12 and 14. Richard has been studying legacy donors for years – and he really knows his stuff!

CHAPTER ELEVEN

Getting to second base

You've succeeded in creating that emotional impulse in Jacqueline's amygdala. She's feeling this urge to make a legacy gift.

She's the right age. She thinks charitable bequests are a good idea. Yours is one of her favourite charities. She has a deep emotional commitment to your cause. She's been supporting you for years and her connection to you is strong. She's warmly remembering why she came to support you in the first instance.

Congratulations! You've reached first base. But there's more to be done before Jacqueline puts pen to paper to make the gift happen.

Jacqueline processes her impulse the way we all do. Her amygdala sends the information to her cerebral cortex. Now the thinking begins. So it's time for you to anticipate that thinking and help her through the gift decision process.

Let's go back to the conventional way of doing planned giving. You've been sitting on Jacqueline's sofa for an hour, sharing wonderful stories about your organization. She's been telling you about her connection to the cause. The two of you are relating big-time. She's even pouring you more tea and offering you another slice of her delicious banana bread.

You've turned the conversation to legacy gifts. You've talked a bit about how they work and why they matter so much to your organization's future. You've told Jacqueline that other donors like her have made bequests. You've suggested that this might be something she might be interested in doing as well.

Then you close your mouth and keep it closed until Jacqueline speaks.

All successful major gift fundraisers have a very keen sense of when to shut up. They know that there comes a moment when they must stop talking – and that the prospect *must* be the next one to say anything.

That's how it's done on the sofa – one-on-one. With Iceberg Philanthropy, you're having this conversation with hundreds – if not thousands – of donors at once. No body language to read. No eyeballs to watch. No intangibles to feel in the air.

Great salespersons and objections

Anyone whose been trained in sales knows all about customer objections. The guy at the car dealership has shown you that model you've been thinking about. He's impressed you with its safety, its roominess and the trade-in price he's offered for your old clunker. You already like the way it looks. They have the colour you want in the show room. It felt great during the test drive and the sticker price is within your budget. You've imagined yourself owning and driving that car and you feel good about the idea.

The salesman senses this and he's beginning to sniff a sale. But then you throw a few spanners into the works:

◈   "My partner wants to get a mini-van,"

◈ "I'm concerned about the gas mileage and the carbon emissions."

◈ "My brother-in-law says that Mazda makes a better car for the same price."

In sales parlance, you've just raised objections. And it's these objections that separate the weak sales guy from the one who pockets the commission at the end of the month.

In short, sales professionals are taught to see customer objections as opportunities – and not deal-breaking torpedoes. The objection is an opportunity to deepen the customer's understanding of the product and appreciate it even more. When the sales person handles objections well, the customer's commitment to the purchase becomes even stronger.

Pre-empting gift objections is a critical part of Iceberg Philanthropy. Let's go there now.

Good news and not-so-good news

We've listened to hundreds and hundreds of charitable donors in focus groups over the years. We've guided them through discussions about their connections to their favourite charities, their attitudes toward legacy gifts in general and how they'd like to have the "conversation" with their favourite charities.

Let's look in on a focus group that's taking place with donors from Save the Pussycats Canada. The discussion has been going on for about an hour. The donors are all warmed up and getting along with each other famously.

The discussion moderator then asks, "Suppose SPC wrote to you and asked you to consider leaving them a gift in your will. How do you think you'd react?"

The not-so good news is that these donors will raise objections – and pretty serious ones at that. The good news is that there are only two objections that come up regularly. Dealing successfully with both these objections is your key to getting from the amygdala first base to the second base of the cerebral cortex. Let's look at each in turn.

"But I'm not rich"

Do you remember Ray Kroc? He's the guy who founded McDonald's restaurants way back in the 1950s. Ray predeceased his wife and when she died, Joan Kroc left a staggering $1.5 billion to the Salvation Army. These gifts make the news. Your donors see these news stories and many of them assume that legacy gifts are the exclusive domain of the rich and powerful.

Remember that Jacqueline sees herself as an ordinary person who does ordinary good deeds. She doesn't see herself as a philanthropist – or a potential philanthropist for that matter. Jacqueline sees herself as an ordinary person and an ordinary donor. She doesn't identify with Joan Kroc in the least.

We suspect that media stories about legacy gifts from the rich and powerful might actually do more harm than good when it comes to donors like Jacqueline. They reinforce the pre-existing notion that charitable bequests are only made by the privileged few.

Here's where there's a disconnect between perception and reality.

The reality is that the lion's share of legacy gifts are made by donors who are very much like Jacqueline. But these gifts don't make the six o'clock news.

The perception is very different. Jacqueline doesn't see herself in the news. The closest thing she might see is the typical story of the spinster schoolteacher who lived a very modest life and then left $5 million to a school breakfast program when she died. This is the "millionaire next door" human interest story. Yet Jacqueline isn't a spinster and she doesn't have $5 million to give away.

So when donors are asked whether they'd see themselves making legacy gifts, the response is often, "I'm not rich enough."

Your challenge is to convince Jacqueline — in a respectful and sensitive way of course — that she *is* rich enough.

This can't be done head on. Please don't go writing copy like, "You're richer than you think!" That just won't cut it with Jacqueline. A more oblique approach is called for if you want your message to stick.

Here are a few ways you can broach the subject and at least get Jacqueline thinking, "Hey, maybe I can do this after all."

- ◆ Openly acknowledge that many legacy donors don't have a lot in the way of cash to throw around. Introduce the idea that legacy gifts come from assets like paid-off houses and cottages rather than from the monthly household budget.

- Remind the donor to think about her home's current value and not what she and Harry paid for it in 1962.

- Tell stories of other people who Jacqueline can relate to. One of our favourites is a man we'll call Cal. He's a 74-year old who was widowed seven years ago. He has a house and a condominium and some investments. Cal lives on a very modest income and makes modest donations to charities that total about $300 a year. A year ago Cal calculated his net worth and was very surprised to learn that his assets totalled almost a half million dollars. That's when Cal realized that he could realize his dream of being a philanthropist by leaving a couple of charitable gifts in his will.

- Stress that gifts need not be in the multi-million dollar range to be meaningful. Make it clear that these mega-bequests are the exception to the rule and that it's ordinary donors (like Jacqueline) who leave the vast majority of legacies to charity.

- Let the donor know that she can leave a fixed amount of money, a percentage (even a small percentage) of her estate or whatever is left over once her other commitments are met. Say this in a way that makes leaving the gift sound less daunting to the donor.

We particularly like residual gifts. This is simply because of asset appreciation and the time lag between the last revision of a will and the death of the donor (often about five years).

We have a colleague in Upstate New York who had a direct mail donor in her database. This donor had made a grand total of two $50 gifts to our colleague's hospital foundation during her lifetime. When the donor died, she left the residual of her estate to the foundation. That residual's value at the time of her death was $9.5 million! Granted, gifts like this are rare and we don't recommend that you broadcast them to your donors. But, if you pay attention to ordinary donors like Jacqueline, you'll probably hit the jackpot every now and then.

Taking a back seat to the family

Let's go back to our Save the Pussycats Canada focus group.

The discussion is progressing nicely. The donors have talked about their giving in general. They've talked about SPC and opened up about why they give and their *donor experiences.*

Then, when they're nicely warmed up, we introduce the idea of leaving a bequest to the charity we're discussing. After a brief pause, someone will say, "I don't know about that. I need to take care of my kids (or grandkids, or spouse)."

Your legacy materials must acknowledge family and the donor's feeling of obligation to "take care of family first." The task here is to demonstrate to Jacqueline that she can provide for her family *and* make a legacy gift.

For some reason, most planned giving materials ignore the donor's family. This is a big mistake.

Before we go into this, it's important to keep in mind that many of your legacy gift prospects won't be thinking of family first. They may never have had children. They might be estranged from children or siblings. So it's important to acknowledge this as well — but obliquely. For example, you might want to say, "We understand that many of our supporters feel the need to provide for family first."

With that proviso though, the majority of your legacy prospects will feel a responsibility to properly provide for loved ones *before* they'll actively consider leaving a bequest to your organization.

The simple objective with your communications is to suggest to the donor that she can do *both* – that it's not an either/or question. You're not competing with the kids. In fact, you're joining them as a member of the group of people and organizations that have given the donor's life meaning and worth.

Here are some ideas and suggestions that might help you deal with this issue.

◆ Talk in broad terms about the donor's life and the legacy she'll leave behind when she's gone. Most parents would no doubt list children at the top of their life's legacy list, but there is room for more. That donor was a member of a community. A neighbour. A citizen. Perhaps an active member of a faith community. A volunteer and a donor who supported worthy causes that strive to improve humanity's lot.

♦ Some donors in focus groups have solved their own problem by thinking of a couple of their favourite causes as "additional children." We're not suggesting you take this literally! But they've said things like, "If I divide my estate into fifths, I could leave an equal amount to each of my three kids, my church and Save the Pussycats Canada." You can do this in your materials by talking about another donor like Cal who approached his will that way.

♦ Don't try to hide your discussion of a potential legacy gift from the kids or grandkids. Encourage the donor to discuss her thoughts on legacy giving with anyone who would help her arrive at the appropriate decision. This shows respect for the donor's judgment and doesn't make you look greedy! Stay on the high road and the donor's opinion of you will go up.

♦ As we've already discussed, remind the donor that a gift like this comes from assets and not income. And encourage the donor to be sure of what her house, cottage and investments are really worth today. Again, telling a story of a donor like Cal gives the donor the opportunity to apply his story to her own situation.

♦ This is also an area where stressing residual gifts or a small percentage of the donor's estate fits nicely.

Safe at second base

If you properly address the issues of wealth and family, you'll really help Jacqueline make the leap from emotional impulse to rational decision. Once she reaches this point, she'll be ready to talk to her family or her financial advisor about making the gift happen.

Send this message to hundreds – or thousands – of the prospects in your database and you'll be well on your way to mining your share of the $15.3 billion that's in the iceberg.

Chapter Twelve
Measure twice, cut once

There's an old carpenter's maxim about measuring and cutting – and we think it applies nicely to Iceberg Philanthropy. Any carpenter will tell you that you can't do it over if you've cut a board too short in length.

This chapter is about preparation and planning – the important work you must do before you spend a nickel or talk to a single donor. Carefully reading the pages that follow and taking them into account as you plan your Iceberg campaign will greatly improve your odds of success.

Fundraising isn't democratic. It doesn't offer equal opportunities to everyone. As you assess your legacy potential, it's really important to be honest and realistic about your organization and the donors who support you. This realism and honesty will help you plan appropriately and execute effectively.

Ready? Here are 12 questions you should answer before embarking on your journey to the iceberg:

1. *How long has your organization been in existence?*

   In most cases, donors will associate your history with your future. They will likely assume that since you've been around for a long time, you'll continue to be around for a long time.

If you've been around for less than 20 years, you might want to take baby steps into legacy marketing. If you have a 20-year history, you should be okay. Twenty to 40 years means that newness won't be a roadblock to your donors' legacy support.

2. Does your organization have a case for support?

We're continually surprised when we come across large name-brand charities that go about their business without a case for support. In fact, this happens much more often than we'd care to admit.

We urge you to ensure that you – or someone in your shop – invest the time and effort in preparing a strong case statement. That investment now will pay off big-time in the future.

It's also important that the case be reviewed through-out your organization and that there is broad consensus that it accurately describes your brand, your past, your present, your work, your impact, your needs and your future.

3. Does your organization have a strategic plan?

Your donors are going to want to hear about your organization's overall direction in their consideration of a legacy gift. Successful charities are often driven by a singular idea that guides decision-making and resource allocation. Unsuccessful charities often lurch from crisis to crisis without a compass guiding their efforts.

Don't let the expression "strategic plan" fool you. We don't want to get into too much detail here, but staff retreats that deal with budgets, fiscal year priorities and staff assignments are in fact tactical planning sessions.

Becoming the leading community hospital in Northern Ontario by providing superlative patient care and eliminating unnecessary waiting times is a strategy. Hiring another administrative staff person to speed up tax receipting is a tactic. The words strategy and tactics are often used interchangeably when, in fact, they are very different creatures.

4. *Consistency vs. change*

As humans we highly value consistency in our relationships. Consistency is considered a hallmark of good parenting. We want our spouses and loved ones to be pretty consistent – at least in the things that matter, like honesty, trust and showing affection.

Your donors are no different. Your legacy gift prospects will have been with you for a while. They're looking to you for consistent messages, consistent program emphasis and consistent results.

If your organization is in a state of constant flux, your donors will no doubt experience some confusion and ambivalence. It's common sense that a confused and ambivalent donor might send another $35 cheque this year. But she's sure not likely to put you in her will!

5. How strong is your brand?

Your brand is your image in the mind of a donor, a consumer of your program/service or even a member of the broader community. When we think of branding, we usually think of logos and graphic design. In fact, the brand goes much deeper than that. Of course, everyone recognizes the Salvation Army's distinctive red shield. But when we see that shield we think of all the dedicated and selfless service the Salvation Army provides to the weakest and most vulnerable in our society. The shield is also associated with personality traits like compassion, unconditional love, tolerance and respect. The Sally Ann is perhaps Canada's best known example of "do unto others" in action.

The Red Cross is another incredible brand. In fact, its value worldwide is ranked right up there with McDonald's, Coca Cola and Microsoft. Despite the tainted blood scandal several years ago, the Red Cross brand is as strong as ever in Canada today.

There are a lot of great books and articles on branding, especially in the business section of your library or large bookstore. Our last word on the subject is. "If it ain't broke, don't fix it!" We often see successful charities change their names, change their logos and change their fundamental message. The effect of these changes is almost always that a once contented donor becomes confused and disoriented. It's a huge mistake to change your brand because your executive director is in a creative mood or because key volunteers are bored with it.

6. *Is direct mail a meaningful slice of your revenue portfolio?*

Thousands of Canadian charities used direct mail to build the base of their fundraising pyramids during the 1970s and 1980s. Direct mail accounts for a significant percentage of their annual fundraising revenue. And direct mail donors make up a large percentage (often a majority) of their donor base.

If this describes your organization, Iceberg Philanthropy is for you.

On the other hand, if you make the bulk of your money from Nevada tickets, product sales and special events, you may not have the right donor base for Iceberg Philanthropy. Remember our earlier discussion of tippers, buyers, donors and investors? Iceberg Philanthropy is all about transforming donors into investors. If your pyramid is based on a platform of tippers and buyers, the Iceberg strategy probably won't work for you.

7. *Do your decision-makers understand today's direct mail market?*

We've already discussed the state of the direct mail market in Canada today. It has begun to shrink (albeit slowly). There is unprecedented competition for direct mail donors and the dollars they give. Costs are edging up and return on investment is inching down.

We still run across frustrated fundraisers who tell us that their boards have told them to "just go grow the program." This lack of understanding leads to poor investments, falling short of expectations and all-round frustration.

It's important that your leadership understand that pushing your pyramid *deep more than wide* is the right strategy for today's market. Once your leaders understand the "leverage" concept, you've cleared a critical hurdle on your way to success.

8. *Is constant staff turnover the norm?*

We've described Iceberg Philanthropy as a long-term process. While your June golf tournament may require six months of work from start to finish, legacy marketing takes a multi-year commitment. It requires a high degree of strategy, discipline and patience to bear fruit.

Achieving this success is made more difficult if the key players in your organization keep changing.

We have several direct mail clients, some of whom we've worked in partnership with for 10 years. One of our biggest challenges today is getting new client staff up the learning curve as to why we run their program the way we do. We had one client for several years that changed the staff person in charge of direct mail on a yearly basis. We're convinced that this constant change cost the client organization money because of their lack of awareness of how things work.

9. *Is your organization financially stable?*

At the risk of being repetitious, Iceberg Philanthropy is the longest-term fundraising investment your organization can make. It will also pay the biggest dividends!

If you work for a charity that's "skating on thin financial ice," your odds of success are lessened. The reason for this is that in the crunch your leadership will find cuts to legacy marketing expenditure the easiest ones to make. The reasoning here is pretty simple. These expenditure cuts can be made without affecting this fiscal year's bottom revenue line (even though the multi-year revenue losses will be huge).

Sometimes people lose their jobs and cash in their RRSPs to pay the mortgage. It's far from the ideal situation, but in desperate times we do what we have to do get through the month. Charities are led by people and those people think the same way when the organization's finances are in trouble.

10. *Does your organization manage its database well?*

Iceberg Philanthropy is an innovative synergy of major gift strategy and direct marketing tactics. Any direct marketer worth his salt will tell you that a direct marketing program is only as good as the database that supports it.

You should have up-to-date donor information on file, including the right form of address (Mr. Mrs. etc.), correct name spelling, current postal address and phone number, accurate giving history (including dates, types and amounts of gifts going as far back as possible) and donor identification number or code.

Selecting the right prospects to start with is critical. So is coordinating legacy mailings with house appeals, newsletters, event invitations and thank-you letters. The entire Iceberg Philanthropy process will yield invaluable donor information which should be kept and used intelligently in the years to come.

Having your database in good working order is an essential prerequisite to success.

11. Do you "work in silos"?

The whole concept of independent and isolated fundraising departments is an obsolete industrial production concept that dates back to the Second World War. When people are isolated in their own departments (like direct marketing, major gift, data entry and research), we call this "working in silos."

Successful organizations today are very *flat* with minimal hierarchy and *interactive* where people talk to each other across departmental lines. The strategy is to make the interaction between the donor and the charity absolutely seamless from the donor's point of view. By the way, donors have come to expect this.

We've had experiences in which Iceberg Philanthropy stalls because the direct marketing manager doesn't want the planned giving department to contact *her* donors. In reality, she cares more about this month's $35 gift than a $20,000 bequest that could be realized in the years to come. This is nothing short of revenue myopia and regrettably it's not uncommon in today's charitable sector.

12. *Do you have the mental flexibility it will take to succeed?*

This question applies specifically to organizations that have already established a planned giving program. Iceberg Philanthropy asks you to take a radically different approach than the one you learned at the Banff School or those CAGP conferences you've been to.

We're not saying the old approach is wrong – because it isn't. Rather the problem is that the old approach doesn't go nearly far enough to reach those ordinary donors like Jacqueline.

You'll be well on your way if your fundraising team is willing

◈   to stay focused on the will

◈   to communicate with passion

◈   to talk to donors about "why" and not "how"

- ◆ to interact by mail rather than face-to-face

- ◆ to tell great stories rather than writing instruction manuals

- ◆ to trust the donor to manage her own finances.

These questions are relative, not absolute. No one answer and no one element of your program gives you an automatic green or automatic red light to proceed with Iceberg Philanthropy.

We offer them for your consideration, each in relation to the other. Perhaps there are a couple of glaring weaknesses from this list that you should fix before starting your program. Others might suggest that you start out a little more cautiously.

You're in the best position to make these judgments and to see the whole picture. You know your cause, your organization, your donors, your leadership and your colleagues. You're in the best place to assess your legacy giving potential.

Do the preparatory work first. Then trust your judgment. We're confident you'll make the right decisions.

Chapter Thirteen
"I won't tell a soul"

You've done it all by the book – well, this book at least.

You've gone through your direct mail donor database. You've identified your most loyal legacy suspects. From that group, you've identified those prospects who love your cause, who are open to making charitable bequests and who have the *room* to name a beneficiary other than spouses and children.

Of course, our Jacqueline is among your prospects.

Then you spent about a year cultivating Jacqueline, using the Iceberg Philanthropy method. She's read testimonials from people like her who have chosen to make your charity a part of their life's legacy. Your CEO has written to Jacqueline and made a compelling case for the need for her support in 15 years time. She's received a newsletter or two full of donor profiles, moving stories and reminders of why she chose to support your organization in the first place.

Finally you sent her a letter asking her to reveal her gift intention – or at least, her inclination. You've popped the legacy question and you wait eagerly for her response.

She's read the cultivation packages with great interest. She feels so strongly about your cause that she truly wants to make it a part of the footprint she'll leave on this world.

Jacqueline has called her lawyer. She's asked to include your charity in her will – to the tune of five per cent of her estate's value. The deal's gone down.

But, dear reader, there's a fly in the ointment.

Jacqueline isn't going to respond to your request that she reveal her intentions to you. Her lips are sealed. And you're going to have to wait, perhaps for a long time, until she draws her last breath and her benevolence is known to you.

Competing interests

Just about every fundraiser we know wants desperately to know which donors are making bequests. The fundraiser has championed the legacy cause within the organization, often competing for scarce budget dollars with the special events team that runs the August Golf Classic and the Viennese Gala. The other guys can show their return on investment. The planned giving officer is frustrated by not being able to lay it all out in black and white the way they can.

In truth, the fundraiser wants Jacqueline to reveal her gift so that the fundraiser can show results for her previous investments and keep the dollars coming for next year's program.

But let's swing around 180 degrees and look at this from Jacqueline's point of view.

Do you remember reading the story of Jacqueline's life earlier? She's a modest woman of modest means. She doesn't like to draw attention to herself. She was raised, by parents who were born at the end of Queen Victoria's reign, to believe that certain things in life are private.

Things like sex, religion, family disputes and politics. People of good upbringing certainly don't discuss death and money in polite company.

We're not just making this up. In focus group after focus group, donors of Jacqueline's age have told us that they would not inform the charity of a bequest decision. When we ask why, they say very matter-of-factly, "It's a private matter."

In other words, dear fundraiser, Jacqueline is of the opinion that it's none of your business.

How many _will_ tell?

When we first started working on the idea of leveraging legacy gifts from direct mail donors, we wanted to employ some best practices from our direct marketing experience. One of those practices is to establish sector benchmarks. And one of those benchmarks we went looking for was "what percentage of bequesters inform the charity of the impending gift?" We looked, and we looked, and we couldn't find the answer.

So we set out to create the benchmark for ourselves. We contacted fundraising professionals from dozens of charitable organizations and we asked them two simple questions:

◆ How many bequests has your organization received in the past three years?

◆ Of those bequests, how many had you been informed about prior to the donor's death?

We had responses from about 30 charities from across the country. They were local, regional and national in terms of scope of work and donor constituencies. We heard from hospitals, international development agencies, advocacy and human rights organizations, disability charities, heath charities, postsecondary education institutions, environmental groups and those in the arts. All in all, we received data from a very good cross-section of the charitable sector.

And here's what we found:

◆ The charities who responded had received a total of 3,004 bequests in the last three years.

◆ Of those bequests, only 253 donors had informed the charity of their gift intentions prior to their deaths. In other words, 8.4 per cent of bequesters informed the charity of the gift. A whopping 91.6 per cent of them kept it to themselves.

So we now have a benchmark we can work with.

You can expect one in 10 bequesters to inform you of her legacy gift decision before she draws her last breath.

Using the multiplier to your advantage

Imagine sitting in your office one morning, tackling the pile in your inbox. It contains a gift intention slip from a donor, telling you that your organization is in her will. You're delighted and you run around the office, telling everyone the news. You explain that this little slip of paper represents a $20,000 gift.

Most legacy fundraisers we know have to work hard to market the idea of legacy fundraising within their own organizations. Receiving a gift like this is certainly an opportunity to have everyone celebrate and for you to drive home the message that this stuff works.

Here's the added wrinkle. You've just told a colleague (or better yet, a boss) about the gift. She's enthused and congratulates you. This is the time to add, "And that's not all! There will be nine more!"

That slip of paper isn't really worth $20,000. It's worth $200,000.

It's important to drive the message home internally – over and over – that for every gift notification you receive there will be nine more gifts in the future.

Can we move the benchmark?

Today, the "notification benchmark" stands at just under 10 per cent. This begs the questions: Can we move it up? Is it possible to convince a greater number of donors to tell us?

The honest answer today is that we don't know, although we have some ideas on the subject. We've begun some research on this subject. Stay tuned for more findings down the road.

Can we move the one-in-10 benchmark? We think so. We suspect that there are two critical messages that Jacqueline needs to hear before she'll consider informing you of her legacy gift decision:

◆ You need to *promise* that you'll safeguard her privacy. Put it in writing. Be explicit. Guarantee that she'll never be approached, harassed or solicited by *anyone* because she trusted you with this information. We don't think that your promise alone will do the trick. But, if you've treated her well over many years, she might trust you enough to tell. You can't change this now. Your organization has either earned her trust over many years – or it has failed to do so. As in any relationship, trust is a sacred thing and it takes time to build.

◆ But more importantly you need to give Jacqueline a compelling reason to tell you. You'll need to make a powerful case. Now making the case for a legacy gift and making the case for revealing a gift intention are different in our opinion.

Jacqueline will make a legacy gift if she believes that her funds will be put to good use for her intended purpose when the time comes. She will only tell you about the gift now if she believes that her disclosure now will further your cause. Your challenge is to do that effectively.

Let's create an example. A teaching hospital could tell Jacqueline that it conducts life-saving research and that many of these research studies take a decade or more to bear fruit. The Chief of Research could articulate how difficult it is to commit to long-term projects like this, given the challenge of securing long-term funding in today's ever-changing world. He tells Jacqueline that if the hospital foundation knew of the gift intentions of donors like her, these important projects can be given the green light – and lives will be saved for people in her grandchildren's generation.

You get the idea. So now you have some hard thinking to do. You need to articulate reasons for donors like Jacqueline to overcome their instincts for privacy. You need to show her that the benefits of revealing her gift will outweigh the cost. In most cases, this won't be easy. But we do think that Jacqueline is a reasonable person who genuinely wants to further your cause.

So do your work. Build your case. We think you'll have some success.

The true challenge

There's no doubt about it. Iceberg Philanthropy offers a blue ocean strategy for visionary and capable charities for the next 20 years. Will your charity use this strategy and reap its benefits in the years to come? Maybe. It all comes down to leadership, we think.

Effective leaders take calculated risks. They're willing to try something new if they've assessed the available information intelligently and weighed the opportunity versus its cost.

We've articulated the Iceberg Philanthropy opportunity as best we can. It's quite simple really:

- 7.5 million Canadians make charitable donations through the mail.

- One in 10 of your donors has already made charitable bequests and more will make them in the near future.

- Legacy gifts from direct mail donors will be worth at least $15.3 billion over about the next 20 years – almost a billion dollars a year.

- The donors who will make legacy gifts to you will do so because they're committed to your cause, have a high level of confidence and trust in you and see your relevance in the future.

- These donors are open to receiving legacy gift information from you and will consider the information if they deem it appropriate and helpful.

- For every donor who will inform you of her gift decision, another nine donors will make the gift and keep the information to themselves.

Our contribution to this effort has been to do the research and obtain the data that makes for a solid case.

We know already that some people will look at these numbers and get to work. Sadly, others will be so stuck in their own red ocean strategy that they can't make the change. They'll keep trying to make more money for their organizations by working harder, even when we know it's working smarter that pays the real dividends. Aren't you working hard enough already? Most of the fundraisers we know certainly are!

We've drawn the map for you. We've put all our intelligence and effort into it. We trust it. The decision to use this map and take a new journey is entirely yours. Should you choose to take that journey, we wish you well.

Conclusion

Some parting thoughts

We believe that fundraisers – be they volunteers or professionals – have a pretty sacred duty.

You have a duty to your organization. A duty to further your cause, whether that cause is caring for the sick in your community, protecting wildlife habitat or providing breakfasts to inner-city kids.

You have a duty to your donors to treat them as the important stakeholders they are in furthering your organization's mission. At the end of the day, it's the donor who allows you to bring your organization's vision to life. They want to find meaning in their giving every bit as much as you desire meaning from your work.

As well, you have a duty to the ultimate recipients of your good work. Your efforts might benefit the poor, people stricken with a particular disease, AIDS orphans in Africa, abandoned kittens or Mother Earth herself. You have taken on the responsibility to make your very best effort to advancing your chosen cause – and making this world a better place.

We wrote this book to empower you to do just that.

You can think of Iceberg Philanthropy as a recipe. We've laid out some rationale, spelled out the ingredients and given direction as to how to combine those ingredients into something truly special, both for you and your donors. As with any recipe, most cooks will start experimenting once they're comfortable with the modus operandi. We encourage you to experiment too. Once you feel you have the fundamentals down pat, you should try to fit Iceberg Philanthropy to your own particular constituency and situation. And you should have fun doing it!

You might think of this book as your legacy marketing template. Templates are designed to save time, effort and money. We hope we've done that for you. This template was put together for you so that you can leverage legacy gifts from your ordinary direct mail donors who up till now have been flying way below your radar. We know from exhaustive research – and lots of trial and error – that your donors are ready for Iceberg Philanthropy. The only question remaining is whether you and your organization can commit to it and make it work.

We see this book as a guide to the future. Direct mail fundraising will be with us for years to come. But it will be increasingly difficult to acquire, convert and renew donors as profitably as you've done in the past. Iceberg Philanthropy allows you to leverage your investment in your direct mail donors – and bring many of them to the decision to make the ultimate gift. What could be more satisfying than to take that donor relationship to this level?

Today's charitable marketplace is more competitive, more demanding, more crowded and more fragmented than ever before. Direct mail is a highly mature fundraising tactic with which you and your competitors wage battle every day. Iceberg Philanthropy offers a new strategic approach that will allow you to break away from the crowd, create some space and be truly innovative with your donors.

Iceberg Philanthropy is innovative because it breaks with the conventional methodology of fundraising. Historically, we've pursued direct marketing with large numbers of donors in the hope of securing large quantities of small gifts. At the same time, some of us have spent considerable "face time" with a select few donors at the top of our pyramid in search of the big gifts.

Iceberg Philanthropy breaks that mould. It allows you to market investment-type gifts to larger numbers of donors than you'll ever be able to meet over tea and banana bread. If you can truly accept the fusion of major gift strategy with marketing tactics, you're well on your way to success. To be frank, some fundraisers can never quite swallow this idea. It doesn't sit well with them because they were trained to do it differently. If you've got imagination and creativity inside you, the Iceberg advantage will be yours.

Iceberg Philanthropy also takes the conventional wisdom as to why people give to a much more fundamental level. It recognizes the simple fact that we humans are – at our very core – emotional and primitive animals. Engagement with the donor begins by creating the *primary impulse* to give. It's only once that impulse has been created that we make the transition to a more rational case for support. In our view, hearts win out over minds just about every time. People who write direct mail copy have known this for decades.

We've also gone to exhaustive lengths to give you a clear and accurate description of the market you'll work within. Your legacy prospects have a definitive profile – one we've personalized in Jacqueline. We can't encourage you too strongly to review her description in Chapter 5 and get to know her as you would know someone in your own family. One key to becoming a great Iceberg practitioner is to allow Jacqueline to rent a room inside your head. In fact, we often find ourselves in conversations where someone will say, "I don't think Jacqueline would like..." or "I think Jacqueline really wants to..."

Jacqueline's been living in our heads for a number of years now. And we've come to enjoy her company.

We hope we've convinced you as to the tremendous potential that Iceberg Philanthropy opens to us. Three quarters of a million donors like Jacqueline have already made charitable bequests. We believe that many more will do so as well, if we follow the Iceberg recipe and approach these donors in a way that resonates well with them. If you remember one number from this book, make it $15.3 billion. That's the minimum that ordinary donors like Jacqueline will leave to charity over the next 20 years. Generating legacy gifts from ordinary donors is truly a new and very exciting frontier. We wrote this book so that you might explore it – and enjoy the journey.

You now know who to start out with. There's an old direct marketing maxim that goes. "Who you mail to is just as important as what you mail." It applies to Iceberg Philanthropy big time. If you begin by applying the *four-legged stool approach* outlined in Chapter 7, you can narrow your focus to those donors who have the greatest probability of leaving a bequest to your organization. Those donors who are the right age, who love your charity, who are open to gifts in wills and who aren't overwhelmed by family obligations — these are the ones you should target, cultivate and solicit.

Iceberg Philanthropy has also given you a couple of very simple, and somewhat contrarian, principles upon which to build your legacy marketing program. These are principles we learned from listening to real donors – much more so than to planned giving officers or allied professionals. Committing fully to these ideas is absolutely key to making this approach work for you:

◆ Stay focused on the will and only the will. Don't confuse Jacqueline with a menu of gift planning options that she doesn't understand and won't use. There's elegance in simplicity. And, fortunately for us, almost all the money is in one place – Jacqueline's will.

◆ When writing to Jacqueline, choose poetry over accountancy every time. Communicate with heart and true passion for your cause. Make her tingle. Make her cry. Make her feel. Remind her why she chose to support you in the first place. Talk about why she should give and let her figure out the how. Jacqueline's pretty smart, you know. She'll find a way to do it if she's truly motivated.

Think relationship. Think courtship. Win her heart – and the money will follow. Love does make the world go round.

There's also a pretty simple method offered in this book. Identify legacy prospects in your database and choose a quantity that fits your capability and budget.

Do some research – some real listening – and let the prospects reveal themselves to you. Take your time and cultivate those prospects properly. Then, when the time is right, pop the question in the right way. Assess your results and make adjustments – and start it up again. Over time Iceberg Philanthropy should cease being a special project and become an integral part of your ongoing program.

Perhaps one of the most valuable parts of this book (at least we hope it is) are the 21 tips on "How to talk to Jacqueline" found in Chapter 10. We encourage you to keep these handy and use them wherever and whenever you can when you're communicating with your direct mail donors. Think of newsletter copy, thank-you letters to acknowledge gifts, web content, new donor welcome kits and general brochures. This list can be pretty exhaustive. But each and every item on it is an opportunity to plant the legacy giving seed in Jacqueline's mind. Doing this doesn't require genius. But it does need disciplined consistency over time. And please do remember the awesome power of a story well told.

We've also tried to help you anticipate Jacqueline's reservations, once her emotional impulse to give has occurred and she starts to think rationally about the ramifications of a legacy gift. American sales guru Zig Zigler preaches that the best way to deal with customer objections is to anticipate them and include them in your sales presentation. We've shared Jacqueline's most likely reservations, and given you some practical advice on how to effectively dissolve them.

It's also important that you take a look in the mirror before embarking on your Iceberg Philanthropy expedition. We believe that most charitable organizations can make great use of the approach outlined in this book. But, as with any other strategic enterprise, a healthy dose of self-awareness and realism is required. While this strategy will work for most, it's not for everyone. An honest and frank review of the 12-point checklist laid out in Chapter 12 will help ensure that you're ready to get the most from your legacy marketing program. We have our mechanics give our cars a check-up before we head out on a cross-country driving vacation. The same idea applies here.

Last, but not least, we've dealt with the issue of gift revelation. An "expectancy benchmark" has been established and, more importantly, we've discussed how you can strategize both to move the benchmark and how to sell Iceberg Philanthropy results to the leadership in your organization.

A closing wish

We hope this approach makes sense to you and that you share our excitement at what this legacy gift frontier offers our causes in the years to come.

We encourage you to stay determined and consistent. Be smart and trust your common sense — because Iceberg Philanthropy is all about common sense! Keep Jacqueline firmly in your mind at all times. Speak to her heart from yours and you will find success.

We wish you well on your journey. We'd love a post-card every now and then to let us know how you're doing. *Bon voyage!*

Afterword

They say there's nothing new under the sun. While Iceberg Philanthropy is a new – and we believe innovative – approach to marketing legacy gifts, it is a recipe that contains many ingredients. We found our ingredients in many different places – from many wonderful people.

- Mike Johnston has been a good friend and partner in our efforts to bring our brand of legacy marketing to Canadian fundraisers.

- Richard Radcliffe has spent years preaching the legacy fundraising gospel – and has pioneered the use of donor focus groups focused on legacy gifts.

- Judith Nichols told us a decade ago to go "deep more than wide" with our donor pyramids in order to maximize the potential of the donors we already have.

- Mal Warwick had the foresight to see the potential of a joint Canada-USA poll of North American direct mail donors – and to probe the potential of those donors to leave bequests.

- David Love has been an evangelist for democratizing legacy fundraising to include those "ordinary" donors in your database.

- Tony Myers and Adrian Sargeant showed us how scholarship and research further the cause of philanthropy.

- Frank Minton and Lorna Somers "wrote the book" on the *how* of planned giving – allowing us to focus on the *why* of bequests.

- Ken Ramsay had the big hairy idea that charities can actually market legacy gifts to large numbers of donors at one time.

- Susan Doyle heard our approach over a lunch in 2003 and simply said "I want to be your first legacy client."

We owe all of these talented people – and no doubt many more – our gratitude and appreciation. We extend our thanks to all of you.

Made in the USA